GW00728041

# ARE YOU READY FOR YOUR INSPECTION

## 2ND EDITION

## VANESSA DOOLEY

Copyright © 2019 Vanessa Dooley
All rights reserved.
ISBN:978-1089699446
ISBN-13

# CONTENTS

# DEDICATION

*This book is dedicated to all those people who are aiming to make a difference in children's lives. Hoping this will give you some further guidance on improving outcomes for children and adding IMPACT.*

*Remember, YOU ARE THE SOURCE!*

# THE WHY!

I have often wondered why people would want to write books, and here I am actually going ahead not only writing one but also writing this revised edition. I would often be in awe of them for containing so much information in their heads that they wanted to get it on paper to share with others. I have also been in awe of the fact they were so knowledgeable and brainy to be classified as authors.

Yes, they are good at what they write.

But this attribute alone does not make people brainy; it, however, does showcase their talent in wanting to share what they know.

So, during my time as a trainer and consultant, whenever the discussion came about as to why do I not write a book, my first thoughts were a combination of the following -

I do not have that much information in my head to write about.

Do I have the knowledge in the first place?

Another one was…. Who, me! The person who left school with only CSEs …yes, I am that old!

…But then, when I started putting pen to paper, I realised, for me, it was more of a mind explosion on paper and so much so that I could not seem to stop.

As a friend once said to me… it is like - your brain dumps all that you know on paper.

So true!

So, once the brain dump exploded, I needed to first lay out and then compile these minuscule pieces of information to create massive pieces of knowledge that would hopefully be of some use and add some IMPACT.

I became excited and thought WOW! All this information was actually inside my head, it needed to be released …not only for my sake but also for others.

This could be of help to people who so often find themselves in situations which have troubled me so many times.

So now is the time for me to share what I know, and from both sides of the coin, so to speak.

## Background

I have always been into Early Years. As a matter of fact, my passion is Early Years … when Princess Diana announced her engagement to Prince Charles - that's when I knew I wanted to be a nanny. It was a craze…not sure why I wanted to follow in her first steps. But it was indeed massive for me to realise that actually there is a job out there that would fit perfectly into my whole perception of meaningful existence. Today, I think I was very lucky to have that thought process very early on... I mean, how many teenagers know what they want to do with their lives when they are at school and take that on earnestly?

The thought of achieving the coveted NNEB was beyond my belief, beyond anything I thought I could achieve in my life. Yet, with the help of amazing friends, supportive husband, children and parents, and the most inspiring Mrs Espezel (yes, we used to call them Mrs in those days), I was able to achieve my ultimate goal.

To cut a long story short, this is where I am today.

I have managed several nurseries and even group-managed six at one time; all achieving the grand outstanding grade. It was a huge role for me and one I am so proud of as it helped me get to where I am today. Without the support of the company owners, I would never have achieved my degree or EYPS; yet another wow moment. Sporting that gown - making my parents and children proud was just an extraordinarily awesome day.

Leaving the group of nurseries was the hardest thing I've ever had to do, but thinking back to that time now, it was the making of the real me. I've always been determined and passionate. I've had this keen desire to see what else was out there, and so I dipped my toes into new pastures and worked my way as an assessor, internal verifier, lecturer, course director for level 2 and 3 as well as the

Foundation Degree, in addition to being an Early Years' inspector.

Little old me, an inspector! And I still pinch myself, thinking how on earth did I get that far. But with the most amazing support from my shadow inspector who I still meet for coffee and cake, I did manage to achieve the pinnacle of my career.

But then things started to change... throughout my time in inspecting, I was always asking the question about training and how settings accessed it, how they self-evaluated their practice. In fact, I remember the staff being petrified when I would turn up to inspect, even though throughout the initial phone call, I would try to make them feel at ease. I vividly remembered what it was like... those sick feelings of what I am going to be asked, how the staff will react to the observations made...what if we have got something wrong, and so on.

One thing I do want to say at this stage is that my husband ALWAYS wished me good luck before I left the house before an inspection. Why? you would ask. Because as an inspector, you are entering someone else's domain, home, pride and joy; and you are on your own. Consider the vulnerability in this scenario.

So anyway, throughout the inspectons, I realised that I needed to get the best out of the setting and the staff. Inevitably, the only way to do that was for them to feel confident in their own setting and shine... yes...SHINE.

This is your one and only chance to show how good you

really are. This is your chance to ensure all the needs of your children, staff and your own self are being met while also ascertaining the level of impact you are making.

The word IMPACT will be a common theme in this book alongside SO WHAT! And it could not have come at a better time with the new Education Inspection Framework adding the words INTENT, IMPLEMENTATION, and IMPACT in the heading of Quality of Education. It is almost like someone 'up there' was looking down on me when I originally wrote this book as well as creating our #JustQuality ADDING IMPACT accreditation. What perfect timing!

If you believe in those types of things – I do and thank you Nan x

During my inspector training, the senior inspector drilled into us the words -SO WHAT – particularly, when we were writing our report. And I have incorporated the use of these throughout my consultancy and training, in fact so much so that I am now seeing those words being used in settings when I revisit them.

So, this is where this book comes into its own. I wanted to share with you the fundamentals of inspection, help you feel empowered and get prepared for your inspection.

There is no manual on this critical event.

Yes, there are books that talk about outstanding practice, there are books that talk about being the leader in the setting. But throughout my research, there has never been an instruction guide, a how-to book, a manual on *how to prepare for your inspection.*

I am not prescribing who this book is aimed at as in my eyes it is aimed at everyone who works in an Early Years setting.

If you are a new manager, this will help to take you through the process from start to the never-ending finish line. If you are an experienced manager, this book will help remind you of those - every day - actions you need to do but do not necessarily have the time for. If you are working in an Early Years setting or as a childminder this book is a great tool to guide you on what to expect during your inspection.

This book will hand-hold you through the journey of the entire process making sure that you are going to shine, you are going to be confident, and you are going to show how you add impact.

During market research, I have always asked this: What is it that you truly want? I've listened, and I've taken this away and put together this golden nugget so that you are prepared for your inspection.

There will be some useful tips; some good practice guides, and some guidance to take you forward in your mission to be prepared.

Throughout the many inspections I have done with Tribal, Ofsted or as part of Jigsaw Early Years Consultancy Quality Improvement Inspections, I have always seen how nervous staff are when walking through the door. I too have been on that end of the spectrum. Through managing many nurseries and group-managing six at a time, I used to dread the knock at the door...the showing of the badge and announcement of the word - Ofsted. These were the days of unannounced visits. I do wish we still had those as we should be adding impact every day and not just for the inspection day. This subject involves a huge debate.

The journey through opening your setting, preparing for your inspection and actually enjoying the inspection itself is no mean feat- trust me on this. My thoughts are impelling me to write down everything I know, to share all my insight. The motto 'sharing is caring' is not only highlighted but also exemplified in this case. You need to shine for others. This book will help you get fully prepared for that day by being consistently outstanding, every single day.

You can make this happen. Let me help you make it happen.

Enjoy the journey and equally importantly, enjoy the process.

Remember, not everyone will understand your journey.

**THAT'S FINE.**

It's not their journey.

It's yours!

# THE JUDGEMENTS

The recently instated Education Inspection Framework is due to be effective from September 2019. It sets out the principles that apply to inspection, and the main judgments that inspectors make when carrying out inspections of maintained schools, academies, non-association independent schools, further education, and skills providers and registered Early Years settings in England.

It might be important to note that we are only focusing on the Early Years within this book. However, the headings are all identical, and correspondingly, the process will be similar.

The Early Years Education Inspection Framework provides a powerful and important tool for parents, as well as carers, regarding the quality of education, training and care. Your inspection results will help parents make informed choices as to whether their child should attend your setting.

If you were inspected between July 2013 and July 2016, you

are now back 'in the pot' and need to be prepared anew for the call. Evidently, it has become harder to achieve outstanding, and maintain that grading, with the goal posts being moved in the new inspection framework.

However, if we consistently strive and work towards it on a day-to-day basis, it will be easier to achieve the grading you desire on the inspection day.

Firstly, let us reiterate, we know that each child is unique. This is very true to your own setting and also to your own inspection. Your inspector will use the Inspection Handbook to judge your setting during several times of the entire day and evaluate your practice.

Use this opportunity to showcase your own ethos and tone without any inhibition. With a continuous, all-out approach, you will be able to maintain your passion to ensure that children are achieving highly. So, when I see on social media comments like, 'I've had the call, THEY are coming tomorrow, what do I need to do?' it scares me! People write different things ranging from, 'My inspector looked at this' to 'Mine didn't, they only wanted to see this'.

Believe you me - your inspector will only follow the guidance, which is the Inspection Handbook, and I cannot emphasise this enough. Your inspector will ask if you have read the handbook and where you would grade yourself using the grade descriptors. As such, against this backdrop, this book will help bring about clarity of the handbook.

Within the new Education Inspection Framework, all areas are covered under the following new headings:

- Overall Effectiveness
- The Quality of Education
- Behaviour and Attitudes
- Personal Development
- Leadership and Management

The four judgements remain the same within the Education Inspection Framework:

GRADE 1 ~ OUTSTANDING

GRADE 2 ~ GOOD

GRADE 3 ~ REQUIRES IMPROVEMENT

GRADE 4 ~ INADEQUATE

Your inspector will make use of their professional judgements using the Early Years Inspection Handbook to clarify and use the grade descriptors to give you a grade at the end of your inspection.

They will also look at your setting, to assess and see what it would be like for a child in your care, with the potential impact on the children's learning and development.

**Outstanding**

If you are judged good or outstanding, your next inspection will be within the next cycle, unless you have a serious complaint which needs to be investigated and could trigger an unannounced inspection. In this scenario, Good to Outstanding settings next inspections could take anywhere between three to four years.

According to the new EIF (2019), 'In order to reach this standard, inspectors will determine whether the Early Years provision meets all the criteria set out under good; for that judgement and does so securely and consistently.'

So, this means that you cannot get some aspects of the judgements in some areas- it has to be all of them. This also applies for the criteria under the outstanding judgement which you will have to meet. So, to reinforce to achieve an outstanding grade you need to achieve ALL of the good statements as well as the outstanding judgements.

With an outstanding grade there will be no recommendations.

## Good or Requires Improvement

These judgements will follow the best fit and your inspector will consider whether the overall quality of your setting is aligned with the descriptors defined in the handbook.

For Requires improvement you will be inspected within the same year.

## Inadequate

You'll be inspected again within the next six months.

You'll be told what you must do to remain registered, and the date by which it must be done. In addition, your local authority will be informed, which may affect your eligibility for funding. Hence, it is critically important to get your inspection right.

You are likely to be inadequate if your safeguarding is

ineffective; or, any one of the judgements is inadequate; or, you are in breach of any of the EYFS requirements, and this will impact the children's safety or well-being or if the setting has two previous Requires Improvements judgements and is still not good.

## Inadequate with enforcement

You'll be monitored by an inspector. They'll visit you to check how you're progressing against the areas you were told needed improvement.

Ofsted may take further action if there's no improvement.

If you have two inspections in a row where you're judged as inadequate, Ofsted can actually cancel your registration.

So, imagine how hard it is to get outstanding and this is the pinnacle of any Early Years' setting.

So, what is it that makes you an outstanding setting?

In all fairness, this question is debatable. However, the Inspection Handbook enables you to use this as an audit tool in order to evaluate your own setting. This is highly recommended.

It is so hard to explain what entails outstanding whilst respecting brevity. So, let us start with the facts.

How do we ascertain what outstanding is and more importantly, how do we ensure our setting reflects this not only on the inspection day but in everyday practice?

I could go on forever, describing what I think it is...but it may well be different from your perception.

I asked this question on social media and not surprisingly, the responses were extremely diverse.

Here are a few examples:

*'Children who are loved and nurtured by every practitioner - practitioners who KNOW their idiosyncrasies and bring out the 'best' in them...'*

**Mine Conkbayir, author and consultant on Applying Neuroscience to Early Intervention**

*'That all the hard work and planning I put into running a safe, warm, and nurturing learning environment for the little ones to flourish and fulfil their individual potential has been recognised.'*

**Jenny Kruk- Strzelecki, Childminder**

*'Engaged children, staff who have the same vision and expectations, reflective practitioners with evidence of reflections, safeguarding as priority with very knowledgeable staff in this area, supportive community for everyone not just children but staff, management, etc. There probably is lots more, but that is some of what I feel it is.'*

**Carey West, Merton Preschool**

As evident from these responses, we all perceive it differently. And, it indeed is.

It is substantially different in every practice. So, how can we show this uniqueness on the day of the inspection? My thoughts are that you can only really show what it is if you are practicing it consistently every day.

This is a FACT.

You cannot just turn up, become outstanding one fine day and demonstrate your ability to do that consistently to the inspector. They will want to see credible evidence of how you've achieved this uniqueness and distinctiveness and equally important, they will be interested to ascertain how you intend to maintain this for the foreseeable future.

No matter how much you think you do not want outstanding and a good would suffice, we all know in our hearts that we're ever so anxious to hear those three magical words during the inspection day.

'You are outstanding.'

However, it is often heard from practitioners that they do not want to get *outstanding*. This is because it is extremely challenging to maintain this grading. At the risk of sounding repetitive: If we ensure achieving an *outstanding* practice every day, it would become like second nature and thus, be much easier to maintain.

Another FACT that must be remembered.

There are many words when writing an inspection report to

describe examples of *outstanding* practice...words such as exceptional leadership, inspiring activities which ignite curiosity, highly reflective - to name a few.

But how do we show this in our everyday practice?

To achieve outstanding, you have to ensure you illustrate and include everything that will help you become outstanding in your everyday practice. There is no point just doing it one day and not on the next. This is not how it works.

Children immediately notice the difference and realise that you are doing things differently when the inspector arrives.

I can give you an example of this. I remember one inspection where a practitioner was taking items out of a carrier bag which she had just bought for the day. She wanted to ensure her Easter activities were the most amazing activities ever.

*This was not the usual scenario with her.*

The children soon realised that they were given an activity, which they had not done before. They actually did not know what to do. They waited eagerly for instructions to be handed over by the practitioner. They were handed pre-cut templates and were asked to stick items around the edges. There was no discussion about the purpose of the activity. And, there was no questioning to ignite their learning from the practitioner either.

Children did not know how to use the glue stick; they were looking at it in a perplexed manner as though they had not seen one before. They were given one pair of scissors to share between three children; however, as the objects were new, they soon began arguing. The practitioner did not interject or explain to the children about the need to share. This soon inflamed into a heated exchange amongst the children and they begin to shed tears. Clearly, the behaviour was not managed effectively and children did not know of any boundaries.

That is not something you want to show on the day of inspection. Needless to say, the *outstanding* grade in such cases moves further away.

So, my advice is to start thinking about your end game right away and you will be able to shine on the day. After reading this chapter, write down five points, defining what you need to do in order to make an outstanding environment possible. Let this be your pledge to yourself. If we write things down, they become a reality.

So, how are you going to get this grade?

This is where this book comes to your help.

**Defining Outstanding**

The extensive task of defining outstanding would take up a whole book, which is not my intention.

The chapter aims to explicate the fact that outstanding means something different to different practitioners, depending on their own perceptions and feelings at any given point of time.

One of the other examples when answering the question, 'What is outstanding?' which stood out in my eyes, is:

*'When I'm standing outside with the warm sun beating on my face and knowing that I have made a positive impact on a little one's life as well as possibly helping a parent understand their parenting duties and overcoming their OCDs.*

*Going to infinity and beyond to help a family and their child/children to develop into fine little people that are ready to conquer the world.'*

**Maimuna Khan, Childminder**

To achieve an outstanding grade, you need to have highly effective staff, in fact, a group that is singing from your own hymn sheet. Every practitioner needs to be providing the necessary tools and ensuring they all meet the unique, innate needs of each child. Your staff need to be passionate and committed to their roles within the team and have a sound understanding of the children's developmental needs. This is so important and often missed.

Many years ago, when I struggled to achieve my NNEB, our setting's 'Bible' was Mary Sheridan. This gave us the framework for all child development levels and milestones from birth to five years of age. We knew it backwards, left, right, and centre. Can you honestly say all your staff know your ethos?

**It is all about the STAFF**

With my background and experience as a lecturer, I have seen students attend because they have to. Not because they want to. This often makes me wonder: Where has the passion for students to want to learn more about children's development disappeared? I know through the many Jigsaw Quality Improvement Inspections, which the Early Years Consultancy has attended, that recruitment is a challenge at the moment and we end up employing staff only to ensure ratios.

Why is hiring reduced to just another tick box exercise?

During my time as an inspector and a consultant, it became increasingly clear that we are using online assessments to inform us of where children currently are in their developmental stage and not taking much notice of whether this is right. So, my first recommendation would be to ensure that all practitioners in your setting have an in-depth understanding of child development.

What does your staff know about the Early Years Foundation Stage?

Do you or your staff know about the ages and stages of development?

Certainly, the inspector would want to see that you are knowledgeable in this area. It is the responsibility of the leader or manager to make sure that all standards are not only met but also kept high – an aspect which should be tangible and visible throughout the day. They need to make sure all their team is on board and able to contribute confidently during the day of the inspection.

At the same time, practitioners need to be passionate and committed to their roles and have a firm understanding of the children's needs. I repeat this point so that you can reflect on this and take a look at the staff within your setting or yourself as a childminder before deciphering what they know about the stage of development of a particular child - and how they are going to achieve their next steps.

Remember you are only as strong as your weakest link!

## It is all about the STAFF

## Audit and Monitoring

Your staff are the pinnacle to achieving outstanding; let there be no doubt about it. They are the significant others who are shepherding children in their journey of learning and development and the onus is on you as the manager to ensure that this is indeed happening.

But how can you guarantee they are?

As well as having an outstanding staff, you will need to show that you are secure in your EYFS requirements through ably demonstrating your willingness to work above and beyond the expected.

You will need to show that children are making consistent and significant progress in all areas. If not, why not and how are you ensuring this is being monitored?

It is the managers'/providers' responsibility to ensure that all the welfare requirements are being adequately met. To that end, use the Statutory Framework for the Early Years Foundation Stage (2017) as an audit tool in order to look at what you are doing under each heading and how this impacts the children within your setting.

If you are a preschool, you may be the manager in place, but you may also be run by a committee.

Let me just clarify this: If you are a committee run preschool, your committee has a major responsibility on its shoulders.

I have been to so many inspections where the preschools are working really hard to demonstrate the impact and ensure that children's needs are being met, but this comes to a standstill when the committee has failed to be compliant in their roles.

This can include not informing Ofsted about new committee members to ensuring their DBS is up to date, or not following the correct procedures for the managers' induction. I just cannot emphasise this point enough: The committee members have got to be fully involved and participative within their setting. They are classified as providers and therefore, need to take on the complete responsibility of the setting. So, if you are a committee-run setting, take a step back and ask yourself this question.

Is the committee fully aware of their duties within their roles?

In case the answer is no, this is the chance to make those changes and arrange a meeting in order to discuss how important this is to the setting and children.

**What is the point?**

Are you reading this and already thinking, 'Wow, there is too much to know, digest and amend in your setting?'

Do you ever get those days where you think what is the whole point?

When was the last time you took a step back and thought – WOW, today was amazing?

Getting my point? Food for thought, for sure!

Throughout my inspection and consultancy, I have been so thrilled to see many settings accomplish for themselves an outstanding rating.

This was their ultimate goal.

Poignantly, the next part of achieving outstanding is to maintain it. So surely, wouldn't it be easier if this was an everyday process and it would be easier to maintain this mind-set and mechanism?

So, what do you need to become outstanding?

**It all starts with a VISION…**

Does your setting have a vision?

This vision not only has to be led by an excellent leader; it also needs to be carried forward by a team that is on board and yes, all the way.

I was once taught by an inspiring leader of a group of nurseries,' Speed of the leader, Speed of the team'.

I cannot stress upon this enough.

We all have an idea of where we want to go and the ultimate goal is to achieve that cherished judgement of outstanding.

*"Your vision will become clear only when you can look into your own heart. Who looks outside, dreams; who looks inside, awakes."*

**Carl Jung**

Starting with your vision,

- Have you ever asked your staff what it is?
- Do your staff team know and live your ethos?
- Why not take this time to ask the question?

*'The highly skilled and passionate management team leads the provision with enthusiasm and dedication. Its vision for excellence is reflected in the highly focused and inspirational staff team. Together they strive to provide a first-rate service for children and their families'*

**Starfish Day Nursery, Oldham**

If your staff are not aligned with your mission and vision, then this, in fact will be potentially the first point of call. Start off with a staff meeting and ask them, what they think it is? It's interesting to hear what their views are, and how good it would be if they came up with an idea that can help in promoting that vision.

A staff meeting could be a way of showing staff that you are prepared to listen, which is so important. I have been to settings where practitioners have said they are not listened to. Showing your team that you have the ability to respect and assimilate their views can have the same positive effect as when we listen to children.

It gives them a feeling of self-worth, a sense of value and the much-needed confidence of sharing ideas. Once you are on board with your setting's vision, this is where and how the goals are set across the team.

What is your purpose for your setting?

What are you trying to achieve and how are you going to get there? This is a great start for reflecting and evaluating your setting which we will talk about in the next chapter.

Communication

*"The art of communication is the language of leadership."*

**James Humes**

The art of effective communication - is this an art?

One of the most important themes of any setting is how a leader or manager communicates with his/her team.

Now is the time to reflect. List the various ways in which you communicate with your team.

Once you have documented this, look closely at each method and think about the way this information is received. Put yourselves in their shoes.

Consider: How often do you have staff meetings? Do all

staff members attend? Do you invite ALL staff members? If no, why not? Can you imagine what it would be like to not be invited to a meeting? Surely, this does not help the entire staff to feel valued or involved.

What about those who do not attend? How can you ensure the entire team is aware of the meeting agenda and have understood the messages being discussed and relayed?

For example; Once I was inspecting a setting and asked a member of staff what they understood about Prevent duty and FGM. The staff member looked at me and said that she was not at the staff meeting when this was being discussed. She then went on to clarify that she does not go to staff meetings as she was 'only cover staff'.

This conversation and her expressions made it abundantly evident to me that she felt undervalued and that she was just there to make sure ratios were being adhered to.

Is that a great start?

Surely, making sure that the entire staff is involved in day to day running of the setting is paramount to achieving an outstanding practice.

Think about this. Would we as practitioners not include all children?

I am hoping you are saying no Vanessa, never. Then why do we feel that we do not need to include the entire staff when it comes to communication?

Now, I totally understand that not everybody can attend

meetings due to other commitments, but then it's important to have that discussion with them to help them feel involved in being part of the team and the mission and vision at large.

So, the next time you have a meeting, think about all the staff and how you can best communicate with them. Think about the minutes of those meetings. Can they be shared with staff via messenger or WhatsApp, if needed? Make them feel part of the team.

If you are a childminder and have an assistant, this open and participative communication is also the key for your type of setting. How do you ensure they all are working alongside you towards your vision?

You need to show that your staff's views are being listened to and taken on board wherever applicable. This demonstrates a leader as being highly effective - a trait which an *outstanding* judgement stands by.

As part of an effective communication system, we need to have the ability to listen to others before we can get our points of view across. We also must factor in peoples' points of view, successes as well as their apprehensions.

> *"The most basic of all human needs is the need to understand and be understood. The best way to understand people is to listen to them."*

**Ralph Nichols**

Having active listening skills within your setting is important to show you are prepared for any change and remain open as well as receptive to new ideas. This, in turn, shows that you are working towards building an *outstanding* setting.

You must be able to demonstrate a coherent vision, determination, and passion for continuous improvement. You also need to be able to consistently reflect and assimilate others' viewpoints, irrespective of how conflicting they are in order to help improve outcomes for children.

After thinking about the way you communicate with staff, think about how you're going to communicate with parents.

- How do you ensure that all communication with the parents is effective and consistent?
- Do you involve all parents?

We will talk about this further in the chapter on Leadership and Management, but it does give you some food for thought. This is one of the key reporting requirements which is needed to ensure the best outcomes for children.

### Focus on the Children's Needs

As a leader, you must show your level of expertise from the very start. You must inspire hope and focus on the children's needs at all times. Their needs are at the forefront of your setting, something that has to be portrayed and felt throughout your entire team. You need to understand and be honest about your journey and know how to take your team through it. At the same time, you need to be extremely reflective and highly engaging in getting things done to achieve the best possible outcomes for children.

Children in your setting need to continually achieve in their chosen areas of learning. If they are not, you need to assess why not, and demonstrate that you are doing everything possible to address the problematic areas.

Notably, outstanding does not necessarily mean all children are achieving highly; it's more to do with how you are ensuring their continual learning and development for each one of them is successful. Remember, every child is unique and has individual needs, which you need to identify and support.

Now it is time for you to reflect upon what you do in your own setting. Go to a quiet, secluded place for about 30 minutes and take an honest look at your setting. I can hear you say in your head as if I have 30 spare minutes for this. If you want to improve your setting, then, certainly this is the much-needed time for reflective practice.

Use the following questionnaire to guide you. Tick the relevant box after you have answered each question.

| Consistently | Occasionally | Rarely |
|---|---|---|
|  |  |  |

*Do you and your staff continually listen to the children and take on board their viewpoints, thus enabling them to progress in the areas of learning and development through their own interests?*

| Consistently | Occasionally | Rarely |
| --- | --- | --- |
| | | |

*Do you and your staff continually enable children to choose their own activities to inspire and ignite their curiosity?*

| Consistently | Occasionally | Rarely |
| --- | --- | --- |
| | | |

*Do your staff members encourage learning in children through the scaffolding of language and questioning?*

| Consistently | Occasionally | Rarely |
| --- | --- | --- |
| | | |

*Are children able to make a choice, able to have a voice and able to choose what they want to do through the various activities in a day?*

| Consistently | Occasionally | Rarely |
| --- | --- | --- |
| | | |

*Do you and your staff enable children to be independent in their personal development skills through a variety of choices and unrestrained freedom?*

| Consistently | Occasionally | Rarely |
|---|---|---|
|  |  |  |

*Do you ensure that in your setting all staff members use relevant and up to date training to develop children's skills and demonstrate its impact on them?*

| Consistently | Occasionally | Rarely |
|---|---|---|
|  |  |  |

*Do you ensure that all children are consistently kept safe through effective risk assessments by ensuring all safeguarding policies are up to date and ALL staff members are aware of the importance of protecting against different types of abuse, radicalisation, and extremism?*

| Consistently | Occasionally | Rarely |
|---|---|---|
|  |  |  |

*Are all staff members aware of any children who are becoming invisible in the setting and interact with those children?*

| Consistently | Occasionally | Rarely |
|---|---|---|
|  |  |  |

*At any point in time, do you find children wandering around the setting looking for things to do?*

| Consistently | Occasionally | Rarely |
| --- | --- | --- |
| | | |

*Are British Values consistently being promoted in the setting among the children by instilling awareness of different cultures and values of other children in the group?*

| Consistently | Occasionally | Rarely |
| --- | --- | --- |
| | | |

*Is partnership with parents continually being supported and do parents have an understanding of where their children are in their areas of learning and development?*

| Consistently | Occasionally | Rarely |
| --- | --- | --- |
| | | |

*Do all parents contribute significantly to their children's learning journey? Do you constantly ensure that all parents (depending on their needs) are working in partnership with you?*

| Consistently | Occasionally | Rarely |
| --- | --- | --- |
| | | |

*Are all staff members aware that the activities they undertake for the children need to have an impact? If so, what is the impact that they are hoping to achieve through the children's learning? Are they able to evidence this consistently?*

| Consistently | Occasionally | Rarely |
| --- | --- | --- |
| | | |

*Are you able to demonstrate that the setting has an ambitious vision?*

| Consistently | Occasionally | Rarely |
| --- | --- | --- |
| | | |

*Do all staff members have high expectations about what each child can achieve? Do they ensure the compliance of high standards of care and the delivery of provision for children at all times?*

| Consistently | Occasionally | Rarely |
| --- | --- | --- |
| | | |

*Do you ensure that your staff is ready to improve upon their practice so that they are able to deliver on teaching and learning?*

| Consistently | Occasionally | Rarely |
|---|---|---|
|  |  |  |

*Do you evaluate the quality of your setting and ensure it is improved through periodic self-evaluation?*

| Consistently | Occasionally | Rarely |
|---|---|---|
|  |  |  |

*Are the views of parents, children, and staff taken into account to impact improvements in the setting?*

| Consistently | Occasionally | Rarely |
|---|---|---|
|  |  |  |

*Do you lead the setting to sustainable success through effective planning and manage the curriculum learning programme to ensure a good start for all the children?*

| Consistently | Occasionally | Rarely |
|---|---|---|
|  |  |  |

*Are children being prepared for school during the next stage of learning?*

| Consistently | Occasionally | Rarely |
|---|---|---|
|  |  |  |

*Do you actively promote equality and diversity and are trained to tackle negativity?*

| Consistently | Occasionally | Rarely |
|---|---|---|
|  |  |  |

*Do you make sure that appropriate arrangements are in place to ensure that all children are kept safe from harm, including prevention against radicalisation and extremism?*

| Consistently | Occasionally | Rarely |
|---|---|---|
|  |  |  |

*Do you make sure that the training is highly effective and improving rapidly through ongoing professional development?*

| Consistently | Occasionally | Rarely |
|---|---|---|
|  |  |  |

*Do you effectively monitor and identify areas where children may be slow to develop the key skills that they are learning?*

Consistently     Occasionally     Rarely

*Do you ensure a highly effective partnership with your parents, as well as outside agencies to ensure that the improvement of provision and outcomes for children is maximised at all times?*

Consistently     Occasionally     Rarely

*Do you ensure you listen to how the staff feels about the workload and ensure they understand where to go in case needed, at every supervision?*

Consistently     Occasionally     Rarely

*Do you ensure there is a highly effective partnership that not only involves your parents but also outside agencies to ensure that the improvement of provision and outcomes for children is maximised at all times?*

Consistently     Occasionally     Rarely

*Do you encourage children to regulate their own emotions and help develop their individual ability to manage their own behaviour?*

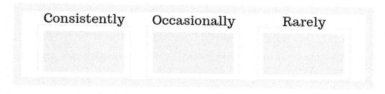

*Do you ensure all children experience the awe and wonder of the which in which they live, through the seven areas of learning?*

*Do you have an INTENT every day? Do you implement the INTENT every day? Do you evidence the IMPACT of the INTENT every day?*

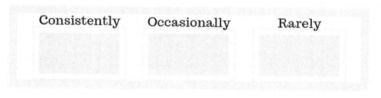

*Do you ensure story time, rhymes and singing are accomplished with excitement and engagement with every child where new words, concepts, and vocabulary are introduced?*

The optimal use of questions should give you a good basis to look at your practice and make improvements.

**Your Practice Is Unique to You**

**The Unique word again!**

To reiterate, your practice is unique to you and you only. Not all approaches or theories are suitable for every setting.

Although having an Ofsted inspection and guidance is highly important for us, they cannot judge us on the way we deliver practice in our setting unless it breaches welfare requirements and as long as we are able to demonstrate the impact our teaching is having on our children's learning.

We need to show that we are providing a welcoming, nurturing and evolving practice which meets the needs and outcomes of each child walking through our door. We need to grow as a setting and discover what works well for us and our children.

You all know your children better than anyone else does. Remember that.

We have a range of techniques, which are ideal as regards our learning styles of children, and we need to ensure that this quality is of the highest form.

By meeting all welfare requirements and the statutory framework for the EYFS, you are well on your way to showcasing your setting. Once this has been achieved, you need to look at your practice, in a step-by-step manner, so as to ensure its efficacy for all children and not just the ones who are exceeding.

**Through the eyes of a child**

Your inspector will want to see What is it like to be a child in your setting. Your report will have a paragraph allocated to this.

Think about putting yourself in a child's body again... can you remember that far back again.

What do you remember... I can probably go back to the age of 5 which for me is around 45 years ago...

some of those memories were not so great and yet some were amazing

This is what the new framework is all about

*What is it like to be a child in your setting?*

From the moment children enter your setting to when they go home

To when they go home and to when they come back to you again.

Throughout this book we will be asking the question what is it like for a child in your setting and what impact it's has on their learning and development

Once you start to use this formula then you will start to be creating a setting which excels in what they deliver and constantly improving and reflecting on your service

So, let's start at the beginning of the day.

What happens when a child enters your setting?

Are they greeted by a member of staff?

Are they asked how they are?

It does not matter the age of the child for we are starting the way we mean to go on with the art of conversation... and sometimes we lose sight of that.

When greeted what do we do then?

Is your setting set out ready for children to start learning and playing or do we encourage children to make a choice from the moment they arrive about what they want to play with? What do you do? And why do you do it that way? What is the impact of this?

Think about this... if you arrived at your hairdressers and they sat you down in the chair and started creating their masterpiece without asking what you would like?

How would you feel?

Insecure, worried, scared?

Whereas if they sat you down and asked what would you like today and listened to your response you would feel valued, and secure that they understood what you were wanting.

This is the same for children.

Encourage children to make those choices, encourage independence and promote self-esteem, self-worth and confidence, what a way to promote resilience.

So, they have started the day with you with good conversation regarding how they are. Think about how you feel when someone asks how you are and actually listens... this is the same for a child... again. The feeling of being valued in of high importance and you are on the right path for children to recognise if they are ok or not. Self-regulation is so important in early years and this is extremely important within this framework. So, think about this.... How do you encourage children to regulate their emotions and feel ok to say they are not ok?

Again, through the eyes of the child this is priority

When it comes to nappy changing or toileting what do you feel a child sees, hears and feels at this transition.

Just picking a baby of the floor while they in flow of kicking, stretching and using their gross and fine motor skills without any recognition of what's you are doing to them is such a no no

Think about what a baby sees and feels... I don't know about you but my knees do not speak, so how do we communicate with babies ... think about eye level, concentration and well as conversation, expression on our faces, the tone in our voices. This is important in a babies time with you in your setting.

When you are changing a babies nappy or toileting with a toddler, talk to them, explain what is happening.

Don't just change their nappy without telling them.

Don't just take them to the toilet without explaining to them why you are sitting them on the toilet.... think through the eyes of a child.

Throughout all my training I have said think about through the eyes of the child and follow a child. Spend that time choosing a child and following them throughout the day

Watch how their key person interacts with them

Watch how other children interact with them

This is so important and the basis of an outstanding setting when you can recognise and improve on what you are seeing with interactions with children and staff.

'Getting it right first time' was published in July 2013 to help with achieving and maintaining the high-quality provision of Early Years. Even though it is over 5 years old, it is still used by inspectors. We should be actively promoting this document in our settings to give us a better understanding of how to get it right the first time.

Areas should be outlined to ensure that settings are aware of what is needed to make a setting good or outstanding. Strong leadership is crucial. It drives up the quality of a setting's work and ensures all children are encouraged to reach their full potential. We will discuss the attributes of strong leaders later in this book.

# WHAT IS THE POINT OF SELF-EVALUATION?

L ast year Ofsted decided to scrap the self-evaluation being uploaded to their portal ready for an inspection.

In Early Years we thought this meant we did not need to evaluate what we do in our setting. This is not the case and it is a reporting requirement for settings to evaluate their practice.

The Early Years Inspection Handbook for Ofsted registered provision (2019: pg15) states:

*'Leaders and managers of settings should have an accurate view of the quality of their provision and know what to improve. They do not need to produce a written self-evaluation but should be prepared to discuss the quality of education and care they provide – and how well they meet the needs of the children – with the inspector. Inspectors will consider how well leaders and managers evaluate their provision and know how they can improve it or maintain its high standards.'*

So, think about how you evaluate your practice and if every staff member in your setting is involved. Evaluating does not mean it has to be all positive, it means the necessary action that you undertake to improve and show how you are adding impact, in case something did not go so well.

Your inspector will have conversations with you and your team about their own evaluation and observe this during the inspection process. They will check to see how accurate this is and observe how staff are teaching, how children are learning, how they are progressing and how the parents' perspective is taken on board, and the quality of your setting.

**Self –Evaluation aka Self-Assessment**

Another term for self-evaluation is self-assessment. So, what does this mean?

> "Self-evaluation will help you to consider the best way to create, maintain and improve your setting, so that it meets the highest standard and offers the best experience for young children." (Page 4 of Early Years Self-evaluation Form Guidance, Ofsted)

We all have different perceptions of reflection and evaluation so when asking the question on social media, the responses were all different albeit with the same meaning:

> *'Evaluating your current position. Reflecting on what else you want to achieve and having ideas on how you are going to achieve these.'*

**Sarah Warne, Childcare and Education Manager, Happy Days Nurseries (South West) Ltd**

*'Not forgetting what you do well as well as areas for development'*

**Anna Wright, Owner Paint Pots Pre-school and Nursery (10 settings)**

*'Reflection of own practice and behaviours, identifying strengths and areas for improvement.'*

**Laura Staff, Teaching assistant/trainee Early Years practitioner, The Arches Primary School, Chester**

Self-evaluation means that we need to look at what we are doing in the present and think about our strengths and weaknesses, and subsequently consider how can we improve on this?

Every day, whether you are an Early Years setting or not, you are evaluating what you are doing and how you would do things differently next time. Consider the scenario when you make your dinner using a recipe. What happens when you serve this at the table and you all begin tasting the meal you have cooked? Do you think it is just fine, or do you often find asking yourself of ways you can make it taste better next time?

Everyone needs to be reflective and evaluate their practice. How else are we going to improve on the way we do things?

Would it be a shocker for you to know that at the end of my inspections, I would often ask the setting under inspection:

How I could improve on the way I inspected?

The look on the managers' faces when being asked that question was sometimes that of pure horror. The question was: Why would you (as an inspector) want to know that?

Here's the thing. Why wouldn't I want to know?

As a lecturer and trainer, we are trained to reflect on every lesson or training. Correspondingly, we should continually ask ourselves what went well and how we can make improvements the next time. If we do not ask ourselves those hard questions, how can we improve?

Ask yourself these questions:

- Can you improve on managing of your setting?
- Can you improve on working in partnership with parents or others?
- Can you improve the quality of education within your setting?
- If yes, how so? Do you ask your staff how you can improve?

Yes, the question is big and complicated but actually gives a real insight into you as a leader or manager. If you are open to change, then this is the way forward. If not, I would suggest you look for another career. Early Years is very reflective and we need to be constantly doing this.

## IMPACT: What does it mean?

So, with that being said, how do we do this to show IMPACT... there is that word again... maybe I should explain the meaning of that word before moving on any further.

Impact here means to have a strong effect on someone or something. So, what do you do in your setting that has an enduring effect on a child's learning and development?

Examples could be:

*The childminder uses photographs of children and their family members on the display board. Children are eager to name and talk about those photographs.*

Based on the sentence above, the impact is that the children are able to feel a sense of belonging and self-worth.

Another example:

*The staff makes accurate assessments through teaching opportunities on a daily basis. Children are able to choose and talk about the dinosaurs in the sand tray.*

The impact of this is the development of children's confidence and speaking skills through their own interests. They engage in questioning-based interaction and use their critical thinking skills to spark awe and wonder of the world.

Back to self-evaluation - whichever setting you are in, whether it is a day nursery, preschool or you are a childminder - we need to do this. Remember, at the beginning of this book I said that you need to shine...now is your chance. Start with your self-evaluation.

Think about how you can show what you do and the improvements you make every day to make sure the children are attaining those high defined outcomes. While Ofsted does say does not mandate you to get this written, but why not kill two birds with one stone and create a document where you can show tangible evidence to parents, visitors, new staff on interviews - as well as your inspector?

Further on within the book, you will be able to read about the new #JustQuality ADDING IMPACT Accreditation which we devised to help Early Years settings demonstrate the several ways which can be adopted to achieve this.

**Versions of Self- Evaluation**

Throughout my travels, I have seen many versions of self-evaluation and that's where the motto of 'Sharing is caring' comes into play. As an inspector, I would always ask about the evaluative quality of the settings. This did not necessarily mean the process needed to be written; however, if it was, it did suggest they were making it a point to record and show whatever they needed to do next. This certainly made a positive difference to the inspection process.

When asked the question: 'Do you struggle to self–evaluate and if so, why?' - The answers were very clear.

*'Time.'*

**Anna Wright, Owner of Paintpots Nurseries, Southampton**

*I think I am constantly evaluating but the recording I*

*struggle with. I have started jotting scribbled notes in my diary bullet journal style and that works for me. It may make no sense to anyone but me but it beats banging my head filling in a template that bears no resemblance to my normal way of doing things just to please the powers that be.*

*When Ofsted come they may or may not like my style but I can talk the hind legs off a donkey about why I do what I do and the impact changes have made so hopefully, that will be enough. I am one little me so I can do no more and I'm good with that.*

**Lynda Hall, Childminder, Basingstoke**

If these are your issues, let's see if we can make this process easier for you.

### Tools on How to Reflect and Evaluate

BE mindful: This is your setting and your time to shine. During your inspection, you will be slightly stressed and probably very aware of your staff, children, parents and even the inspector on the day. So let us use the self-evaluation to say the following:

**What?**
**So What?**
**Now What?**

Thank you, Driscoll (1994) for providing us with this simple tool of how to reflect and evaluate.

This means (i) looking at what you do, (ii) what was the impact, and (iii) thinking about what you are going to do to change it in order to improve. My suggestion would be to break the sections into areas where you are being inspected, as this will ensure that you cover each section.

For example:

Another way of evaluating is by using IMPACT sheets. These can be used for every day or every week and placed in a folder where you are able to see how you are improving.

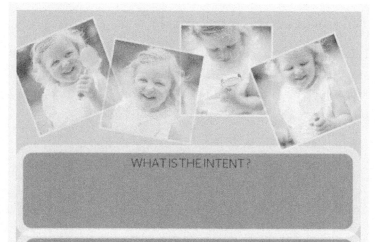

WHAT IS THE INTENT?

HOW ARE YOU GOING TO IMPLEMENT THE INTENT?

WHAT WAS THE IMPACT OF THE INTENT?

Jigsaw Early Years Consultancy 2019

This is one example of good practice:

Have you ever felt you wanted to further accentuate the strengths of your setting? So, why not develop a scrapbook idea which makes it possible for each section to be evaluated on a weekly basis?

Divide the scrapbook into the following sections:

- Quality of Education
- Behaviour and Attitudes
- Personal Development
- Leadership and Management

This is an example of how you can evaluate with impact, and please feel free to add more parameters in order to customise it to your setting. For instance, if you are a day nursery, consider giving your settings' rooms their own learning journal to showcase what they do well and the things they can do to ensure children are continually developing.

This would not only help with your whole evaluation process in your setting; it would also give the team a chance to be involved and take autonomy of their room. In turn, this would make sure that all your staff members are on board with the whole process as opposed to leaving this to you as the owner or manager.

See the last chapter for more ideas!

# THE CALL

*The best preparation for good work tomorrow is to do good work today.*

**Elbert Hubbard**

H ow do you feel when you get the call?

- Anxious
- Scared
- Nervous
- Irritable
- Excited

Why do you think? Is this how you feel? Is it because this is your first inspection, or because you have had a bad experience before? Or does the word 'inspection' make you feel this way.

Regardless, you need to showcase your setting throughout the process. This is your one and only chance to demonstrate the construct of your setting and staff; and the underlying principles to the Ofsted inspector. I cannot stress this enough to you. Every activity from this day has an IMPACT on you, your staff, your setting, your children as well as your parents. Which is why it is so important to think every day is an inspection day!

When will you get that chance again?

Remember, the inspector is a human being too, who has a family at home just like you and me - and is only doing his/her job! They want children to achieve the best outcomes and can only judge you based on the time they are with you.

With that in mind, SMILE, it will and does make the day go better.

So, think about when answering the settings phone during the day. Is it usually chaotic and the noise is carried through to where you are answering the phone?

Do you ever think 'I will leave the phone to ring and I am sure they will ring back?' Yes, people usually do. But one word of caution: The inspector will only make three phone calls to try and make contact with you. If you do not answer the phone on each of these three occasions, they are well within their rights to arrive unannounced!

The inspector will usually call the day before around lunch time...yes

I know that is your busiest time. We have devised this chapter to make you well prepared and confident when the call is made.

**Preparation Is Key**

If you are a childminder, the call will come approximately five days before your inspection. You will be asked your availability for the next five days in case you have Early Years children.

First impressions definitely count, so make sure that whoever answers the telephone knows how to respond to 'That Call.' Do you have a standard way of answering the telephone? Think about how first impressions are made when you do.

The inspector will explain that they are visiting you the next day (or within the next five days if you are a childminder) and inform you about their arrival time. Make sure to ask their name. This is so important as it will set you at ease and this will also set the tone of the inspection.

**Typical Questions on the Call**

At this point, you will be asked questions and it would be good to have the information readily available.

Some of the questions will include:

- How many children currently do you have on roll?
- How many children would you have on the day of inspection?
- How many staff do you have working on that day?
- How many children do you have with EAL?
- How many children do you have with additional needs?

- How many 2-year-old funded children do you have?
- Do you have any children with EYPP?

## Prompt Sheet

We have provided you with a prompt sheet, which will ensure that you are thoroughly prepared to answer these questions.

### READY FOR THE OFSTED CALL

DATE OF CALL:

TIME OF CALL:

NAME OF OFSTED INSPECTOR:

NAME OF ADDITIONAL INSPECTOR IF ATTENDING:

CAR DETAILS INCLUDING REGISTRATION

DOCUMENTS NEEDED:

1

2

3

4

5

6

TIME OF ESTIMATED ARRIVAL:

ANY OTHER INFORMATION NEEDED:

INFORM PROVIDER/OWNER

**Points to Remember When You Get A Call from Ofsted**

- Try and find a quiet place to receive the call
- Remain calm
- Be polite and professional
- Stay positive and your confidence will shine through
- Ask for their name and record the details
- Ask for their car details as this will help with any car parking issues, in case, there is a space constraint in your setting
- Ask them if they require lunch. Usually, an inspector will take some time off to eat their lunch, particularly when the inspection is a day-long process. This gives them and you some time for a breather. They are human after all!
- Ensure your documentation is ready for the day of inspection

**Documentation Checklist**

We have prepared a documentation checklist which you will need to have ready on the day of inspection.

Being prepared for this will make it easier for you to stand out whilst also enabling the inspector to spend more time with the children and staff to make observations.

This will help you to excel, look confident and organised.

Checklist of documents needed for inspection

| | |
|---|---|
| Current staff list and their qualifications, including paediatric first aid certificates | |
| A register/list showing the date of birth of all children on roll and routine staffing arrangements | |
| A list of the children who will be present at the setting during the inspection (if not shown on the register) | |
| The Disclosure and Barring Service (DBS) records and any other documentation summarising the checks, vetting and employment arrangements of all staff working at the setting. | |
| All logs that record accidents, exclusions, children taken off roll and incidents of poor behaviour | |
| All logs that record incidents of discrimination, including racist incidents. | |
| A complaint log and/or evidence of any complaints and resolutions | |
| Safeguarding and child protection policies | |
| Fire-safety arrangements and other statutory policies relating to health and safety | |
| A list of any referrals made to the designated person for safeguarding, along with brief details of the resolutions | |
| Details of all children who are an open case to social care/children's services and for whom there is a multi-agency plan. | |

**Informing the Setting**

Make sure the whole setting is aware that you are expecting an inspector, including staff members who might be absent on the day of the call, or the intimation meeting, but are supposed to be working on the day of the inspection.

Remember the motto: 'Speed of the leader Speed of the team', all team members need to feel valued and made to feel that they are as much a part of this journey as you are.

Gone are the days when the inspectors would simply arrive on your doorstep unless it's a compliance visit. There is much debate over whether such unannounced check visits are right or wrong. I have been on the receiving end of both and can safely say that the stress of knowing inspectors are coming is far greater than the stress of opening the door to them.

The whole purpose of the call is to clarify the registration status of your setting and any changes made to the registration. These are duly noted and you will need to produce evidence that you have notified Ofsted about the changes on the inspection day.

As an inspector, the most common faux pas I have experienced is with committee run pre-schools. The number of times I have arrived at a setting, having pre-checked the portal for the names of nominated persons and committee members, only to find changes on the day. However, Ofsted never received any notification. Note, any change is a reporting requirement.

The chair of committees needs to realise the importance of informing Ofsted of ALL changes. This includes the EY2 form. Failure to do so will definitely impact the grade of your inspection, even before the inspector goes any further to see what a great job you do.

An example of such a report would read like this:

*'The provider failed to ensure that the relevant information about new committee members was sent to Ofsted to enable them to complete suitability checks.'*

The provider in this case, as it is a Committee run pre-school, is the Committee. I cannot stress how important it is for the Committee to understand that they need to have a secure knowledge of their setting.

This could lead to a Grade 3 (Requires improvement) or Grade 4 (Inadequate) rating, as this discrepancy will impact the safeguarding requirements.

**Check prior to Inspection by the Inspector**

Before the inspection, the inspector will check the following:

- They will check the registration of your setting and confirm the same with you. In case of any ambiguity, the inspector will cross check with their regional duty desk and try to resolve the issue promptly.
- They will confirm all pieces of information regarding the individuals connected to the registration.

- All information relevant to your setting is stored on their database.
- Any lines of enquiry will be shown on their portal; this includes the recommendations based on previous inspection, any safeguarding concerns and any complaints that may have been recorded. These would also be shown on the portal and the inspector downloads these details before visiting you. Only Ofsted has access to this information.
- Any previous reports submitted and prepared in connection to your setting.
- Any published information such as any monitoring letters sent out to you. They will check your website in case, you have a website.
- If you have a social media page, the inspector will check the page. Please be very mindful of the regulatory due diligence for all the information you upload on your page. For instance, if you are showing the faces of children, the inspector will want to confirm that you have secured written parental permission.

Please do remember that your personal page does have a linkage to your business page. Whatever is put on your social media page will be shared worldwide. Think about how this may look to the general public.

You will also need to speak to the parents and inform them that you are having an inspection.

Parents need to be given the chance to speak to the Ofsted inspector. As one of the reporting requirements, this is indicative of a good working partnership. Your inspector needs to be able to write how well you work with parents and others. If your parents are unable to talk to the Ofsted inspector, why not ask them to write you a testimonial?

It all builds to the body evidence and forms part of you evaluating your practice (see Chapter 2).

**Tips for the day of inspection**

- Do not panic
- Be prepared
- Breathe
- Remember through the eyes of a child
- Remember that you know your children well, you just need to explain the same to the Ofsted inspector. They do not know the children at all, so will want to know what you know.
- Think about if the Ofsted inspector was asked to be the key person to your children instead of you on a particular day; would they know which stage the child is at based on your quality of teaching and children's learning.

This is a really important aspect to be aware of… all children need to be observed, assessed, and planned for at all times. There should be no gaps in their learning.

**On the day**

When the inspector arrives, they will introduce themselves and show their identification. In case they do not, please ensure you ask to see their credentials. Also, if you wish to contact Ofsted to confirm this, you have every right.

The inspector will then inform you of the plan of the day. They will also want to:

- Check the accuracy of the information they have on your setting.
- Gather any information regarding staff absences, and details such as how many children you have on roll.
- If you have not placed the notification of inspection on your entrance, then please ensure that you do, so parents and visitors are able to view this.
- Agree on the timetable for inspection activities, a walk around the setting, joint observations and any trips or visits that would be happening during the day.
- Allot time to speak to parents – this may be first due to the timings of parents visiting the setting.
- Allot time for Leadership and Management Walk and talk.
- Check staff qualifications and record them as evidence.
- Arrangements for feedback – any other individuals you wish to be present.

If you have an unannounced inspection, your inspector will refer to any concerns (which may have been recorded in the previous visits) that have led them to inspect your setting without being notified.

On some occasions, you will be inspected by two inspectors. There are a few reasons for this:

1. The main inspector may be having their Quality assurance visit by a senior inspector.
2. The main inspector is being shadowed by a new inspector in training.
3. The main inspector will need to have a few inspections under their belt before they are signed off as competent.

Treat these inspectors as you would any inspector. Shine throughout the day.

With the new Education Inspection Framework starting in September 2019 there has been much conversation regarding the amount of data that should be gathered and collated in each setting. Please be mindful of this and demonstrate you know where your children are in their ages and stages of development. See the chapter next on Quality of Education for more details and guidance.

# QUALITY OF EDUCATION

Previously known as Teaching, Learning, and Assessment, the Education Inspection Framework (2019) has changed to Quality of Education. The reason behind this was because Ofsted felt this was overly reliant on outcomes and the supporting data which we had to produce.

Please be mindful, this does not mean that data is taken away. Think about how you can evidence the starting points for a child, or his current stage.

Throughout this chapter, we will focus on what your inspector will want to see and what they will do to make sure you are having an impact on children' s learning through your teaching.

I have still retained several subheadings from the previous Teaching, Learning, and Assessment, however, I have used also used segregation into relevant sections using new aspects within Quality of Education.

## 3'I's and Cultural Capital

The main changes within this chapter refer to the 3'I's and the introduction to Cultural Capital.

The Quality of Education is now broken into three different aspects which the inspector will want to see.

These are:

**INTENT**

**IMPLEMENTATION**

**IMPACT**

So, with this in mind, we will break this down further so you are fully aware of what you need to know.

Firstly, let me just reinforce this to you. Each of those aspects, the 3 I's are not being graded separately. Instead, inspectors will reach a single grade judgement for the Quality of Education, by gathering all the evidence they have seen, using their professional judgement.

In addition, using their professional judgement, the inspector will also consider the ages, development, and stages of children in the setting.

Whatever you do please do not get hung up on this formula – It is an amazing formula that works and it will help you see the whole purpose of why you are doing what you are doing? In fact, so much so I personally believe if you took this to the other areas you will have the most perfect evaluation tool. (See the last chapter.)

**INTENT**

This is all about what you want children to learn. What is the purpose of your teaching? What is the curriculum (EYFS), which you want the children to learn and develop?

Every day, you have a plan for each child on what you want him/her to learn. Every day you have a plan of what you want to teach the child. So, use the child's plan to enhance your plan and meet the collaborative end result- the impact.

Whether it is to encourage a child to be independent in their self-help skills, using scissors, pouring their own drinks, understanding more mathematical concepts, increasing their vocabulary – there is an intention every day.

## IMPLEMENTATION

This is all about how you implement your curriculum, that is, the EYFS?

How are you ensuring that children are making progress in all of the seven areas of learning?

This will draw from the intention you had earlier. So, in context of the intent, consider how you are going to implement this, what and how are you going to get the children to achieve this? Are you going to create an adult-led activity to see if a child can use scissors, develop pouring skills using the sand and water tray, create a mathematical shape hunt, read a story and engage with further sounds to increase children's vocabulary?

## IMPACT

So, you have implemented your intention – now what?

This is the best aspect!

What IMPACT has this activity, this intention had on children's learning and development? Was there a result?

What was the result?

Needless to say, there does not need to be a result which is positive! Yes, this is where your intention comes a full circle and you think about what and how you want a child to reach that intention.

How do you evaluate the impact of the curriculum you are teaching? How do you find out what children can and cannot do?

How do you assess their knowledge and development levels and stages?

This is a cycle of events, which will help you and children evaluate their achievement. Think about, SO WHAT!

Was is the purpose of your activity and how can an IMPACT be achieved and what is its result on children.

Inspectors will observe and have conversations with the

leaders to find out the intentions of the settings and if they are being met. They will want to know if these intentions are adequately comprehensive and challenging enough for children.

Inspectors will want to see how you use any additional funding, which does include the Early Years Pupil Premium and measure the impact on disadvantaged children's outcomes.

At various platforms including draft consultation, Ofsted seminars and conferences, it has been expressed that data will be minimal in the new framework. I cannot stress enough, this does not mean to stop tracking your children, it does not mean to stop assessing, only because this term has been removed from the title of this area.

Think about this - How else are you going to know where a child is in their learning if you do not know where they started from, how else are you going to know what is their next stage in learning? Please do not stop tracking! It is the only way to demonstrate your awareness of the child's development with an accurate idea of the learning level and development stage.

**Effectiveness Assessment**

Throughout the day, the inspector will judge the effectiveness of your Quality of Education by evaluating the extent to which:

a) You are able to show what a child is able to achieve in

your setting. This must also include children who are not exceeding in their development. If they are exceeding, your inspector will want to see that you are continually demonstrating that the child is making progress and that you are working proactively to ensure that they do not fall behind in their development.

b) You are able to show to the inspector that you understand the age group you are working with. Conversations will be oriented towards finding out how well you know your key child and what is the next stage of their development - Your INTENT, how you are going to IMPLEMENT your intent.

c) Baseline assessments are taken from when a child starts, which includes parents' views and other providers such as preschools, childminders and day nurseries that the child may have attended.

d) The assessments you are writing for the child are used to plan for the next stage of learning; this is able to identify children who need extra support in order to help them do well.

e) You are able to show how you interact and encourage children to facilitate their development using questioning and critical thinking.

f) You are able to show how parents understand the progress of their children and how they can contribute and support their child's learning.

g) You are able to show you recognize diversity and encourage equality of opportunity throughout your learning and teaching at the setting.

h) You are able to prove that the teaching you are incorporating helps children secure skills and develop/learn successfully. This will ensure they are able to be ready for school.

Throughout the day, the Early Years inspector will want to see how effective your teaching is to ensure the growth and development of children using the characteristics of effective learning.

The key evidence that you will need to show is how well children are:

- Playing and exploring
- Being active in their learning
- Being able to think critically and create

You will need to show how you evaluate your teaching to support children's learning and ensure that you are aware of the stages and ages of your children in your setting.

*'Children's learning is meticulously planned and is informed by the regular and precise assessments of their development. Staff constantly reshapes activities to help children to develop their concentration skills and to motivate them to keep trying. Staffs are skilled and confident in knowing when to allow time for children to lead their own learning.'*

**Little Learners, Corby**

Your inspector will want to observe how children interact with each other, including with you and your staff, as well as how this will impact their progress.

**Progressive Check**

This does include the Progress Check at 2, parent contributions, and also the summative reports which are shared when children leave for school. From your assessment in your setting, the inspector will want to see that you are able to plan effectively and encourage the traits of effective learning. They will also want to see the impact of your staff's qualification, knowledge, training along with their own learning and development. The quality of all activities in each age group will be considered on the basis of their efficacy.

- So, when a child starts with you, what do you do to gather all the right information?
- Do parents and key people complete *all about me* form which asks for details to explain the child's interests?

- Do you encourage parents to highlight where they think a child is in their stage of learning?
- If so, how do you do this and what IMPACT does it have on children's outcomes?

Your inspector will want to see any evidence gathered from children's starting points and this can also be gained by talking to both practitioners and parents about the level of children's social, communication, and physical skills upon entering the setting and how these are observed when they are still new into the setting.

The inspector will use this evidence to evaluate how well you know about and understand the progress children are making towards the early learning goals. The inspector must judge whether the adults' expectations for children are adequately defined whilst also seeing how confident you are in children's development.

In addition, the inspector will want to see children who are disadvantaged and those who are under-achieving or are catching up quickly. How do you monitor and ensure this is happening?

How to ensure that this is being assessed and written correctly? How often do you evaluate the checks?

The Early Years Foundation Stage (EYFS, 2017) requires that parents and carers must be supplied with a short-written summary of their child's development in the three prime learning and development areas of the EYFS:

- Personal, Social and Emotional Development
- Physical Development
- Communication and Language

This happens ideally around 2 years 4 months and its purpose is to support practitioners, parents as well as other outside agencies to see where a child is and enable early identification of any developmental needs so that additional support may be sought.

You need to remember that there is no particular format which needs to be recorded, but only the information which needs to be provided for the prime areas.

**Aims of The Progress Check**

- Enable you as a practitioner to understand a child's needs and effectively plan for them.
- Review a child's exclusively in the three prime areas.
- Provide parents with a clear understanding of their child's stage of development.
- Enable parents to support children at home to enhance their learning.
- Support your intentions with optimal actions to ensure the children achieve their milestones.

The Progress Check at 2 should be completed by the key person who should know the child really well. They must use their observations in the setting to assess the stage of the child's knowledge, how they understand what they are learning and their behaviour - whilst also considering the views of parents as well as other practitioners such as the inclusion office, if necessary, in the setting.

You will need to explain to the inspector what you do with this information and the details of the information network.

So, think about this information.

Who do you give the report to? Is it just to the parents or carers of the child? If it is why do you only give this to either one of them and not both?

Every child has a Health Visitor who also completes a check at 2 which is recorded. What impact would it have if you sent a copy of the progress at 2 not only to parents but also to the Health Visitor? This is an excellent way of demonstrating how well you work in partnership with others and would serve as a great example of explaining to your inspector that you are proactive enough to work with others at all times in order to meet the needs of children.

If you have any children with additional needs, you need to be able to demonstrate how you are supporting the progress of these children. This is again a very important point. All outcomes need to be consistent in all areas and if not, you will need to explain why not and what/how you are intending to improve upon these.

Children who speak English as an additional language need to be able to gain the skills they need to communicate effectively. Again, think about how you do this in your setting, what is your intention and the impact of how you implement the intention.

Your inspector will evaluate the children's outcomes and take account of children who have made typical progress (or more) from their starting points. An example of typical progress for a child would be that they consistently display the knowledge, skills, and understanding appropriate to their age. They would also be moving steadily towards the early learning goals, which is evidenced through your assessment records of those children.

Children who commence at a lower level of development than is typical for their age should be seen to be able to catch up and make steady progress. A child joining the setting at a higher level of development than would be typical must be given challenges to deepen their learning; this personalised individual achievement is very important.

Every child needs to be focused on by their key person - and assessments, observations and activities need to be able to show that you are meeting every child's unique needs.

Through the day, the inspector will want to observe children's learning and the way staff members interact with children throughout each of those activities.

I have decided after much focus on the new framework to still retain details about Teaching, Learning, and Assessment as it comes under the umbrella of Quality of Education to give you a better understanding of what is to be expected during the inspection process.

Things to remember during your inspection day:

The Early Years inspection handbook for Ofsted registered provision (2019: pg 33) states in the outstanding descriptors,

*'The provider meets all the criteria for a good quality of education securely and consistently.*

*The quality of education at this setting is exceptional.*

*In addition, the following apply.*

- *The provider's curriculum **intent** and **implementation** are embedded securely and consistently across the provision. It is evident from what practitioners do that they have a firm and common understanding of the provider's curriculum intent and what it means for their practice. Across all parts of the provision, practitioners' interactions with children are of a high quality and contribute well to delivering the curriculum intent.*
- *Children's experiences over time are consistently and coherently arranged to build cumulatively sufficient knowledge and skills for their future learning.*
- *The **impact** of the curriculum on what children know, can remember and do is highly effective. Children demonstrate this through being deeply engaged in their work and play and sustain high levels of concentration. Children, including those children from disadvantaged backgrounds, do well. Children with SEND achieve the best possible outcomes.*

- *Children consistently use new vocabulary that enables them to communicate effectively. They speak with increasing confidence and fluency, which means that they secure strong foundations for future learning, especially in preparation for them to become fluent readers.'*

Clearly, consistency in everything you do in your setting. You cannot achieve *outstanding* unless you are consistent with your exceptional practice across all of your rooms, all of your staff as well as in engaging all of your parents.

Think about this... You are only as strong as your weakest link. Every setting has a weak link and I highly recommend that after reading this you focus on that person. Firstly, let me get this straight. Being weak may not be because they are just not engaging as much as you would like them to. This may mean they need extra training, they may be shy, they may not feel confident in their role. It is your job to help them to grow. FACT. That is indeed the manager's job - To improve on staffs' ability to help children achieve the best outcomes.

**Evaluation Checklist**

Here is a checklist to help you at your starting points with your own setting.

| QUESTIONS TO ASK YOURSELF | ALWAYS | SOMETIMES | NEVER |
|---|---|---|---|
| Do you have a balance of adult-led and child-led activities? | | | |
| Are children being asked open-ended questions? | | | |
| Do your staff give children enough time to answer a question? | | | |
| Are staff making eye contact when children eventually answer the question? | | | |
| How do you evaluate your activities? | | | |
| Is this being evidenced to show IMPACT? | | | |
| Are children given a choice of where, when and what they can play with? | | | |
| Can children easily access open-ended resources to enable critical thinking skills? | | | |
| Are children being encouraged to be curious and independent learners? | | | |
| Do practitioners encourage children's interests and include their experiences? | | | |
| Do practitioners encourage children to try new things and be able to learn from their mistakes? | | | |
| Are practitioners confident about observing, assessing and planning for children's next stage of learning? | | | |
| Do practitioners encourage children to support each other to achieve a goal? | | | |
| Do practitioners know how to motivate children and have high expectations of them? | | | |
| Do practitioners show enthusiasm and full engagement with children? | | | |
| Do practitioners model language which encourages children to think and prepare for next stage of learning? | | | |
| Do practitioners make the opportunities for 'teachable moments' and record these effectively? | | | |
| Do practitioners observe the levels of engagement children have in their room? | | | |
| Do practitioners fully understand the needs of the babies and their care routines? | | | |
| Are key people aware of children's next steps and are these age appropriate? Can staff talk about where their key children are in their learning? | | | |

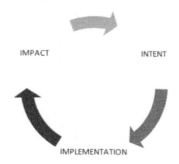

IMPACT       INTENT

IMPLEMENTATION

Invest an entire day (today) to look at the activities that you are providing and setting up for your children. Taking this time will help you reflect on what you have and what you need to change.

- Do you have an intention of the day?
- Do you know? If and how you are going to implement your intention?
- Do you feel you can improve upon the intentions?
- How do you evaluate your activities and your continuous provision or your environment?
- What was the impact of the activity?
- Do you get all staff involved?
- Do you get the children involved?
- If not, again what is stopping you?

Children need to be involved with their setting. They are the ones that are learning throughout the day. If you are not questioning, facilitating, investigating, communicating with children to extend their learning, then you should be thinking:

Is this the right job for me?

Your inspector cannot show they have preferred practice when they inspect and cannot offer any advice. This was one of the areas I found hard when I was inspecting. I could give recommendations but advice throughout the day was frowned upon, and this led to the establishment of Jigsaw Early Years Consultancy Ltd.

As long as you are showing that the things you are doing are having a positive impact on children's learning and development, you will be good.

There is much debate about how we should plan. To be able to plan 'in the moment' for children, you need to get the basics right first. The Statutory Framework for the Early Years Foundation Stage (2017) states:

*The **learning and development requirements** cover:*

- *the **areas of learning and development** which must shape activities and experiences (**educational programmes**) for children in all Early Years settings*
- *the **early learning goals** that providers must help children work towards (the knowledge, skills and understanding children should have at the end of the academic year in which they turn five)*
- ***assessment arrangements** for measuring progress*

*(and requirements for reporting to parents and/or carers)'*

The term teaching can sometimes be contrived as a formal way of working. It covers a wide umbrella of ways in which practitioners can help children learn. During some of my inspections, I have had conversations with childminders who say they are not teachers as I have briefly mentioned before but I am afraid that this statement is not quite true. As parents, we are teachers and as practitioners we are teachers; yet, we are also facilitators.

We facilitate children's learning and play through planned and child-initiated activities. We model our language and communicate with them by demonstrating, explaining, showing, exploring, investigating, encouraging, recalling as well as setting and extending challenges.

We need to take account of the resources we provide, the environment and surroundings as well as the structure of the day. When thinking about the resources, we need to be able to provide a host of different textures, shapes, sizes, and resources that are interpreted in terms of whatever a child wants them to be. It is all about the process and not the end product.

The whole point of them being open-ended is that they can become a whole new world for a child. This can be a struggle for the practitioner as they have only known what they know based on their past experience. Think about this.

Take a real apple – write down everything you can to

describe the apple and questions to ask about it. When I did this training with my delegates, the number of questions was in the high 40s.

Now take a plastic apple – Cross off any questions from your previous list which you cannot ask about the apple you now have. How many questions do you have now?

Now take a printed picture of an apple – Cross off any questions which are not suitable for the picture. How many questions do you have?

This type of exercise is so important that encourages you to think about the resources you have in your setting. The more open-ended resources you have, the more thought-provoking questions, critical thinking skills and creativity is being used by children.

Think about our brain for one second. Think of it as a muscle. Just like any other muscle, if we do not use the brain it will waste away.

This is why we need to ensure that we are providing the most effective form of teaching as possible to help children learn and develop. You are the source!

**Sustained Shared thinking**

A good definition of sustained shared thinking is as follows:

*'Sustained shared thinking' occurs when two or more individuals 'work together' in an intellectual way to solve a problem, clarify a concept, evaluate an activity, extend a narrative, etc.*

*Both parties must contribute to the thinking and it must develop and extend the understanding. It was more likely to occur when children were interacting 1:1 with an adult or with a single peer partner and during focussed group work.'*

## The Effective Provision of Pre-School Education (EPPE) Project (2004)

This gave us a better understanding of the concept called sustained shared thinking. The provision also highlights its significance and how it is fundamental to use this practice as practitioners through our teaching so as to ensure that children are learning.

When a child becomes absorbed in a conversation with a practitioner or their interests are captivated during an activity, this will ignite their learning, use their brain, and provoke further investigation. Children will want to discover more and with the help of you as the facilitator, the learning will begin. The story will begin to unfold and children will begin to ask questions amongst their peers.

Whether it is one to one or with a small group, sustained shared thinking can be a powerful tool to provide a connection between all. This, in turn, forms a relationship where children feel nurtured and secure. Opportunities arise to reveal a level of cognitive development, boosting both self-esteem and self-worth. The feeling of being valued is of utmost importance to a child. Hence, personal, social, and emotional well-being is one of the prime areas. We need to get this right and then learning will begin to flow as it should.

The theories about sustained shared thinking contributed to the original EYFS, which explicitly stated that sustained shared thinking should be an integral part of a child's creativity and critical thinking (EYFS 4.3). It is also indirectly described in **all** the areas of learning and development.

When you are planning for children's activities, ask yourself: Do you specifically look at areas they need to be developing and create activities which are aligned with that area of learning?

Why do you do this?

Think about your time and what you want the child to learn.

Throughout my inspections, I have seen activities being facilitated which only cover one specific area of learning. Think about how time-consuming this is and what is it that the child can get from that activity. Or are the zones perfectly labelled to cover all areas of learning? Think about why you do this? If you do this, is it for your benefit or the children's? Do the children develop more with those labelled zones? If not, why do you have them?

It is not an Ofsted requirement for you to have labelled areas. If it is for rich print environments think of other ways you can achieve this? Books for example!

Why not try this at your next staff meeting?

Give an item to each person - only one item and see how they can link it to the different areas of learning. This will not only help with observations but will also make you and your staff think about the activities you are offering and how these can impact your children's development.

Let us take the example of a pen. Brainstorm and write down ALL the areas of learning for which the pen can be used. I use this example in my Quality Improvement Inspections and highly recommend you do this at your staff training. Use the form below to help you with this training exercise.

This will be a good staff meeting exercise to encourage staff to think outside-the-box. The more this is done, the more practitioners will be aware that everything we give a child can encompass all areas of learning.

Things to remember during your inspection day:

EIF (2019) stated in their good descriptors:

*'Practitioners understand the areas of learning they teach and the way in which young children learn. Leaders provide effective support for staff with less experience and knowledge of teaching.*

Think about the following when you are preparing for your inspection.

- Have you planned for all seven areas of learning?
- How are you developing your practitioners to become experts in children's development and learning?
- How do you ensure that the environment is suitable for the age and learning stage of each child?

- How do you ensure that children are engaged consistently?

Inspectors will want to see how you evaluate your teaching in your own setting. What is the IMPACT of what you are doing?

**Peer on Peer Observations**

To work on Quality of Education you do need to work on Quality of Teaching.

Do you perform peer on peer observations?

I would highly recommend that you start performing peer on peer observations if you haven't already. This will not only help when you are eventually observed on the inspection day but will also go a long way in ensuring that you are evaluating your staff practice and making recommendations to improve.

In order to make peer observations successful, all practitioners need to be fully involved and be willing to reflect on their own practice. The practitioner does need to have a responsibility to take constructive feedback once the observation is complete. Feedback needs to be given when there are no children around and an ideal way would be to link with staff supervisions.

**Key points of Peer observations**

- Acknowledge your skills, celebrate strengths and recognise your knowledge

- Encourage you to identify areas for your continuous professional development
- Give you accountability to improve your practice
- Empower you with new ways of working
- Develop a professional relationship with your peers. (I would highly recommend you perform peer observations on each other if you are a childminder; this is exceptional practice)
- Enable you to upskill your practice
- Use the information as part of your supervision process
- Provide reflective evidence for Ofsted and your setting's self-evaluation

See the example below

**PEER ON PEER OBSERVATION FORM**

EVALUATION OF PRACTITIONERS PRACTICE

| Observer | | | | Practitioner observed | | | | |
|---|---|---|---|---|---|---|---|---|
| Room | | | Date | Time | | | | |
| Focus of observation | | | | | | | | |

| Grading Criteria | OUTSTANDING | 1 | CONSISTENTLY | | | | |
|---|---|---|---|---|---|---|---|
| | GOOD | 2 | MOSTLY | | | | |
| | REQUIRES IMPROVEMENT | 3 | SOMETIMES | | | | |
| | INADEQUATE | 4 | NEVER | | | | |

Add up the scores at the end of the observation to see where the practitioners practice is

| | 1 | 2 | 3 | 4 |
|---|---|---|---|---|
| Does the practitioner engage in a conversation with children | 1 | 2 | 3 | 4 |
| Does the practitioner watch and observe children before they engage in conversation? | 1 | 2 | 3 | 4 |
| Does the practitioner talk at an appropriate rate and make eye contact? | 1 | 2 | 3 | 4 |
| Does the practitioner listen and respond to children? | 1 | 2 | 3 | 4 |
| Does the practitioner model language well? | 1 | 2 | 3 | 4 |
| Does the practitioner encourage children to express their thoughts and use new words? | 1 | 2 | 3 | 4 |
| Does the practitioner encourage independence and confidence in children? | 1 | 2 | 3 | 4 |
| Does the practitioner encourage children to speculate and test ideas through trial and error? | 1 | 2 | 3 | 4 |
| Does the practitioner enable children to explore and solve problems? | 1 | 2 | 3 | 4 |
| Does the practitioner behave as an excellent role model? | 1 | 2 | 3 | 4 |
| Does the practitioner support children to recognise and respond to their own physical needs? | 1 | 2 | 3 | 4 |
| Does the practitioner attend to childrens personal needs? | 1 | 2 | 3 | 4 |
| Does the practitioner praise the childs achievements? | 1 | 2 | 3 | 4 |
| Does the practitioner provoke curiosity and critical thinking using open ended questions? | 1 | 2 | 3 | 4 |
| Is the practitioners body language warm and welcoming? | 1 | 2 | 3 | 4 |
| Are children engaged fully in their play? | 1 | 2 | 3 | 4 |

ADD UP HOW MANY IN EACH GRADE DESCRIPTOR

| | |
|---|---|
| OUTSTANDING | MOSTLY 1'S |
| GOOD | MOSTLY 2'S |
| REQUIRES IMPROVEMENT | MOSTLY 3'S |
| INADEQUATE | MOSTLY 4'S |

**TARGETS TO IMPROVE**

DATE TO ACHIEVE BY :

Now we have finished focusing on your teaching practice, let us move on to the way children learn.

During the time your inspector is with you they will want to see how children are read stories, how they sing rhymes and how this helps with their communication and language. What we suggest is you just observe how your staff do this with children. Using these observations create your own story time and rhyme observation sheet

- Does the practitioner maintain eye contact when reading to children?

- Does the practitioner introduce the story?
- Does the practitioner sit at the children's level to make eye contact when reading and singing?
- Does the practitioner encourage participation from the beginning of the story?
- Does the practitioner model language well?
- Does the practitioner repeat words for children to copy?
- Are all children engrossed and engaged in the story or rhyme time?
- Does the practitioner use open-ended questions to create curiosity?
- Does the practitioner ensure all children are involved?
- Are children bored when practitioner is reading or singing?
- Does the practitioner change her voices and tones to engage children fully?
- Does the practitioner give children time enough to answer questions?
- Does the practitioner encourage all children to be involved?
- Is the practitioners body language warm and welcoming?
- Are the stories and rhymes age appropriate?

**Learning**

Inspectors will ensure that they are able to evidence the following: Characteristics of Effective Learning through the characteristics of effective teaching. This is paramount to a child's journey within your setting.

They will want to see that children are able to play and explore their surroundings, be active in their learning and are able to think critically while also being creative. Children's outcomes will be met through the art of effective teaching. The impact of your teaching will ensure that you have a secure understanding of children's learning. Through the quality of your activities, you will be able to show that children's development is paramount to everyday practice.

We know that teaching, learning and assessment is collectively referred to as the observation, assessment and planning in the learning cycle. But how effective are these in your setting? These should intersect and work together to demonstrate a tangible IMPACT on children's learning. We cannot effectively do one without the other.

It is a bit like a Jigsaw puzzle.

You can have all the pieces placed on your table, but it's what do you do with them that eventually matters.

Do you put the pieces around the outside and then start completing in the middle to make the picture? Or do you randomly take a piece and try and find another that will fit with the one which is in your hand!

**Reflective Practice**

Like a puzzle, you need to have a method to implement your intention- your plan.

Can you honestly say that you do all three aspects of this

cycle effectively and are able to maximize impact within your setting? Are you able to show how effectively children are learning through your successful teaching? This self-assessment and review need to be constant throughout your setting, in each age group to build any chances of achieving good or outstanding.

I have been a part of many inspections as an Early Years Inspector and then as a consultant through our Quality Improvement Inspections. During which, I have noticed that the three areas do not always work in conjunction with each other. This then fails to reflect your teaching in the children's learning and within the assessments you are writing. Again, if you are not showing any impact this will affect your overall grade.

If you are not able to show how effectively and consistently you are demonstrating impacting, stop and think why is that?

What do you think is the reason for this?

- Is it a time issue?
- Is it a training issue?
- Is it a monitoring issue?

Or is it all three?

We need to ensure that our practice is reflective and realise that we can improve upon how we deliver to ensure the children's needs are being met constantly.

There are four overarching principles which are able to shape our best practices.

- Unique Child
- Positive relationships
- Enabling Environment
- Children develop and learn in different ways and at different rates

As well as the four principles and getting the basics right you also need to make sure that you are covering **all** of the seven areas of the Early Years Foundation Stage

**Areas of The Early Years Foundation Stage**

**Prime areas**

Personal, social and emotional

Physical development

Communication and Language

**Specific Areas**

Literacy

Mathematics

Understanding the World

Expressive Arts and Design

So let us go back to the basics and talk about the most important

- the UNIQUE child.

The understanding of these principles of EYFS is paramount in understanding how a child learns best. We can follow several approaches to help us with the best practice, but it is highly important for us to understand that we cannot implement these approaches without taking into account the needs of our children. Each child in your setting is unique.

They all have different learning styles, and their needs are different from each other. Each child has different interests and develops in a unique way. We need to take into account this first before planning our children's learning journey to ensure that we have covered the bare necessities.

Take the time now to reflect upon each child. Use one week to formally not observe, assess or plan for the children in your care; instead, take a step back and follow them everywhere they go.

- Do they have a particular interest in an area of your setting?
- Do they have a schema?
- Do they prefer to be hands-on or just sit back and watch?
- Do they like to get their hands dirty or do they prefer not to partake in the creative activities you have set out?
- Do you need to set out and assign activities, or are children able to choose for themselves?
- Do they encourage their peers to be involved in their play?

This activity is very important to get to know your children and I highly recommend undertaking this activity when you have new children starting with you. Observe their cycle of learning and make notes. This record will help you plan for them eventually and knowing their style can help you out when your inspector asks you to explain about a particular key child. They will want you to tell them everything and demonstrate that you understand their learning journey.

Use the time this week to extensively focus on this. Just one week.

It will not make *any* difference to the assessments of your children; in fact, it will have a positive IMPACT on their learning. Because this exercise will help you gain a better understanding of them as a child.

Carry post-it notes and make intelligent notes of your key child's interests. This will give you a sound basis of knowing what unique means to children within your setting. Use this information to start being the facilitator in the children's story of their time with you.

Once you have the information, observe and record after one week.

Use the first observation after this week as a baseline for where (the stage/level) you think your children are in the learning and development cycle. We will discuss this further in the understanding of assessments.

**Positive Relationships**

Your inspector will want to analyse the relationship you have with children within your setting.

Positive relationships between staff and children are able to give children a feeling of belonging and a sense of self-worth. Relationships need to be warm and loving; the practitioner needs to be ultra-sensitive to a child's needs. They are encouraging, supportive and consistent with their boundaries. These relationships are a clear way of providing ground for heart-felt and stimulating conversations wherein the practitioner becomes a facilitator for the child's needs.

The inspector will want to talk to the children's key person and ask them to talk about a particular child they are observing. They will want the practitioner to know the child's interests, where they currently are in their stages of learning, and what are their next steps. They will also want to observe these steps in day-to-day functioning, to assess if these are impacting a child's learning. This is highly reinforced within the Education Inspection Framework.

The Early Years Foundation Stage (2017) explains that practitioners would do well to be sensitive to a child's needs and respond sensitively to extend their learning and curiosity. By a practitioner observing and tuning in to a child, they will be able to discover what the children like to do, when they are confident in their surroundings and when they are in need of extra guidance.

Effective learning can only be demonstrated when children are being motivated. With motivation, they will begin to show signs of concentrations and will engage in a meaningful play where they are able to use their critical thinking skills, learn from their mistakes and become resilient.

Equally, effective learning can only be determined when

practitioners are able to model active listening skills. To that end, the use of eye contact and responses to a child's discoveries begins to have significance.

Think back to when asking a question to a child. How long did you wait for an answer?

Giving children adequate time to answer a question not only ensures that they have a feeling of self-worth, but also encourages their brain to process and respond more effectively to the question. If you keep asking a barrage of questions, the children will tend to only remember the last word you shared with them. It is imperative that practitioners show respect to children and let them learn for themselves in their own unique way.

It is often said that the environment is the third teacher. This idea was postulated by the schools of Reggio Emilia, who opined that the experiences learnt within your environment hold the key to the successful development of the children. Providing resources for children to participate and collaborate with their peers whilst also being facilitated by the practitioner is paramount to holistically embedding learning in a child's day.

Think about your environment and take a glance at areas where children are actively learning. The use of observations will be immensely helpful to evaluate how your children are learning, and which areas are being enthusiastically used and constantly developed by children within their own play and learning. Moreover, open-ended resources are highly effective in a child's day and as such, need to be actively promoted. Encouraging the children to use awe and wonder to create curiosity in order to develop their own critical thinking and skills provides the basis of vital learning.

Generally, children are born curious and the one thing we all know that in today's society; personal, social and emotional development is high on the agenda of any learning. In order to foster their curiosity, children need to explore the world around them and an open-ended environment gives them just that. It has no pre-determined boundaries and there is no fixed outcome. Children are also able to follow their own imagination and enable their creativity to take them wherever they want to go. Indisputably, this is paramount for learning to take place.

Children learn best through provocations which you provide for them. Over the past few years, the word provocations have been spreading like wildfire.

Do you know what this means?

Firstly, the term originated from the Reggio approach. Put simply, provocation means provoking learning by enticing children to play and encouraging them to be curious, creating awe and wonder to think for themselves. These, in fact, entail all the characteristics of effective learning which we need to aim toward and ensure become known to us within our children's everyday learning.

Now, it is tempting to think that you do this day in and day out by making your setting inviting and enabling children to share their interests; however, these resources need to open-ended so that children can decide what they want to do, how they want to do it and when they want to do it. Remember children learn more during a process rather than with an end product. However lovely it may be, children need to feel their learning is being valued through their own processes.

Are we being too adult led? Again, another debatable question. But the fact is children learn best when they are interested in what they want to do, not by what you want them to do!

**Curiosity Led Creativity**

In The Art of Thought, Wallas (1926) suggests four processes for curiosity led creativity:

- **Preparation**
- **Simmering/ incubation**
- **Illumination**
- **Verification**

**Preparation** – when we are being creative, we investigate all areas.

**Simmering/ incubation** – creativity can drift two ways - positive and negative - and it's up to the artist to find helpful solutions by using the brain.

**Illumination** – after the above two stages, the A-ha or Eureka moment eventually occurs.

**Verification** – is in creating the creation!

Linking to provocations, we should be making sure that our activities are interesting and original to the child. They need to find for themselves the direction of their choice to make it their original learning. The key here is all about keeping it simple.

Try it. Visit your local scrap store and place the resources around your setting. Do not assign any activity, simply sit back and watch what happens - think about what Wallas has suggested. The art lies in provoking communication and language to get children to think for themselves!

Your inspector will not want to be able to take into account the different approaches or ethos you have in your setting, but they do need to see what a child is learning within your setting.

Think about this.

You can use two tin cans.

Can 1: Is labelled stating what is inside of it. (Tomato soup, in this exercise)

Can 2: There is no label. It is a plain silver tin can.

Which one of the above is going to provoke more curiosity, creativity, critical thinking skills, investigations, discovery, and exploration?

The next time you set activities out for children, use these questions as a tool for your staff:

- What area of learning are children achieving with this activity?
- What skills will the children be using?
- Will this engage and excite children?

- Will this provoke imagination and spark inspiration?
- Will this be a good basis for children to take the activity off to something new?
- What is the IMPACT of the activity?

The involvement in children's learning assumes topmost priority for them to learn. Indicators of such involvement give us vital clues of how children are learning. This self-learning process starts at a very young age – from the time they are babies - where connections to the brain grow and join together to form other connections. Without this, children will not develop.

Emotions, regardless of whether they are positive or negative, have an impact on the way children learn. Negative emotions will not encourage brain neurons to join and will create stress and anxiety in a child's life. This will adversely impact their learning, whereas positive experiences in a child's life will give them the desired hunger to learn more and ensure their life's trajectory is moving forward.

Children have an eagerness to learn and be curious. They delight in being investigators and are able to discover new ways of learning. It is all about the learning process for them, and not merely the desired end-product.

I have been to several inspections where I see end products of what children have created.

Think about this!

Have children produced the Mothers or Father's Day card?

What impact did this have on their learning? Why did we do these activities?

Children need to be able to process what they are doing, and this can only be done by allowing and rather facilitating the children to be unique in their own learning. Worksheets are another example of a product of something which the children have not been the original supplier.

Pieces of artwork should be from a child's own perspective and not from ours. It should not be because parents want to see this end result. When you show parents around if you explained to them why each piece of artwork will be individual, this will surely show you are treating each child as their own.

Again, they are UNIQUE.

The point of process over product is that there is no right or wrong way. There are no step-by-step instructions or samples for children to follow. They are able to show their own meanings and there is no right or wrong way to explore or create. The pieces of art produced remain highly focused on the child's experiences and exploration of tools, material, and media.

The whole process will be calm and children will spend

much longer creating their own masterpieces. It will be the child's choice. Your inspector will want to see how you are encouraging this type of learning. They will also want to observe the children making choices with confidence within their surroundings. They will want to see practitioners facilitate this style of learning and be able to share their findings with the inspector.

**English as an Additional Language**

Children who have English as an additional language is currently a hot topic. The inspector will want to see the opportunities you offer to the children to develop and be able to use their home language during their play and learning. In addition, activities should be devised which also support their native language.

The language used in a child's own home needs to be developed in your setting within their learning and development. Much research from Chomsky explains that children learn from their home language early on and are able to extend this learning during their Early Years.

Within the Education Inspection Framework (2019), it states,

> *'Practitioners ensure that their own speaking, listening and reading of English enables children to hear and develop their own language and vocabulary well. They read to children in a way that excites and engages them, introducing new ideas, concepts and vocabulary.'*

Your inspector will want to observe practitioners reading stories to children – an exercise, which will create an excitement for language in them and encourage them to remain focused. They will want to observe rhymes and songs to introduce new vocabulary and repetitive words to extend their understanding and learning.

So, look at your staff, are they all good at creating story time and being engaging and inspiring, if not why not? I would highly recommend when you have new staff come for an interview to do a role-play for you or ask them to read a story to some children and observe. Use the observation sheet below to help you make the decision on whether these are the right practitioners for the children in your setting.

Correspondingly, what are we scared of when any child is starting in our setting? Are we scared of getting it wrong or not knowing what to say?

During an inspection - early on in my inspection experience, I was able to observe a child enter the pre-school and just wander around. I chose this child as I clearly fathomed that he was nervous and zoomed straight to the sand pit.

I observed and recorded his activities for two hours. During that time, he did not move from the sandpit; he did not play with the sand, nor did he build anything. His hands were just placed within the sand and he was gazing around the room.

This child did not have English as his first language.

After evidencing my observations, I requested to speak to his key person. They did not know the child's next steps or where they were in their areas of learning. I inevitably got concerned about him. I explained that I had been observing this child for a long period of time and did not find anyone talking to him.

The practitioner looked at me and said she did not know what to say to him as he did not speak English.

Yes, I am still surprised today as I write this, do you also find this alarming?

So not only was the setting aware that English was a second language for the child, but they also did not know what his next steps were as observations were neither accurate nor recorded effectively to show where he was in his learning.

I asked how they would have felt if no-one spoke to them for two hours. If not one person acknowledged their presence, how would that make them feel? The limited communication and language support for this child surely did not prepare him for school which he was supposed to start within the next few months. Interactions from the staff remained poor and also showed that the opportunities for learning and engaging in worthwhile activities were limited.

Needless to say, this setting did not achieve a positive grading.

Children's home language is very important to provide those critical family links, especially if you have children who are being cared for by older, non-English speaking family members. Between the children and their carers - they need to be able to have purposeful conversations with each other. And as a childminder, it becomes your responsibility to ensure this.

## Assessment

Throughout the day, the inspector will want to see how you know what a child needs to learn what you have observed? You need to see what has taken place throughout a variety of processes such as examples of children's work through mark making, evidence from any photographs you may have taken, and discussions from parents about things you have not observed before.

Your inspector will want to see where a child was when they started with you.

These are referred to as starting points or baseline assessments.

Practitioners need to ensure that the content, the sequencing and the progression in the areas of learning are secure and that you are demanding enough of children.

Whenever I have visited settings and asked to see the children's starting points, there has been no consistency in the records. It constitutes a good practice to enable a child to settle in your setting before you set out to track a child.

However, you can observe visually from Day one and a highly efficient practitioner will begin to build a picture of the child starting from the initial time. They will also start to see a child's likes and dislikes whilst analysing the way they are learning. This, in turn, will ensure that children's unique ways are being taken into consideration during their development.

As part of the starting points' process, we also need to gather information from the parents. How do you do this in your setting? As mentioned previously, parents are the first educator and gaining this information is paramount to working in partnership. The information gathered when a child starts with you can be a good way of gathering much useful information. Using 'All about me' documents as part of the settling in time and gathering at home visits begin to set up a clear picture of a child.

This is such an important time to tell parents how often you will be observing and assessing their children - and how important it is for them to equally contribute. On their part, parents will want to know who is their child's key person; and this early engagement will start to form the much-needed relationship in Early Years settings.

It is also a good practice to ensure that you are meeting the needs of a child and that their starting points are assessed within the first three-week period maximum. This will give you adequate time to take parental contributions into consideration. Using the areas of learning, the key person should be able to make a judgement from their observations to decipher where a child is working within and identify the stages of learning and development through a 'best fit' judgement.

Use the headings

- Beginning

- Developing

- Secure

These will help you prepare the first chapter of a child's journey and ensure that you are meeting their particular needs.

In addition, exceptional practice would be necessary to make sure this is consistent within your setting. Now, for the inspection, think about how can you demonstrate this?

If you are a day nursery, one way that I recommend within my own Quality Improvement Inspections is to complete a Starting point or Baseline assessment at the point of entry to each room. This will not only ensure that children's assessments are kept up to date, but also prove that practitioners are consistent in applying their knowledge of children's development.

**Formative Assessment and Summative Assessment**

Through the practice of consistent observations over a period of time, the children's own learning story will start to evolve. In companionship with the use of your provocations, invitations and the facilitation of their play, this will result in progress and planning for the next steps. This is called the assessment of learning and is based on the information you need for everyday planning. It is also called formative assessment.

Another form of assessment is called summative assessment. This is written by summarising the evidence you have collated from the formative assessments over a period of time. This information is further condensed to share with parents and outside agencies, towards demonstrating the progress of children.

If you do these, think about when you write these at this particular time.

The inspector will want to see how you do this and its impact on the children's own learning journey.

Providing this type of assessment is paramount when working in partnership with parents as this serves as a reference guide. This documentation informs them of which stage their child is currently in and how they can help ensure that they are developing, or if any intervention is needed.

A good idea to share summative assessments is at the end of each term. If practitioners start to give evidence of their understanding of where a child is currently situated, then this will show that they have good knowledge on how to develop and provide the requisite tools for the next stage of learning.

It is important to show you can prove how well versed you are with the uniqueness of each of your key children and their progression to the inspector.

Inspectors will want to find out where starting points are for the child as well as their individual progress. The corresponding evidence must ensure that you are aware of any additional needs and how you are going to ensure these do not have any adverse impact on a child's learning journey.

In a group setting, the inspector **must** track a sample of two or more children across the inspection. The inspector will discuss with you regarding your learning plans for those children, and what they already know and can do already.

This evidence will be gathered by the following:

- The practitioners' knowledge of each child
- The progress check for any child aged two
- The impact of any Early Years pupil premium finding on a child's development
- The quality of support for any children with SEND
- The discussion helps with each child's key person and how they decide what to teach
- How well children are developing in all areas of the EYFS that helps them be prepared for their next stage of learning including school

It is highly important to make sure the job of tracking is effective.

Think about the observation cycle and the Jigsaw pieces we discussed earlier. You cannot have one without the other.

Whichever way you assess children, whether it is paper-based or using online journals, you will need to show your inspector how confident you are in child development. You will need to know what your key child's next stage is in learning and underpin this plan with adequate reasoning.

By ensuring that children are being taught inspirationally, you can ensure that they are successfully learning. Through the success of their learning, you will be able to assess effectively. It's a cycle, please understand, and you need to show the impact you are making.

**Child Development Tracking**

No doubt, Ofsted inspection and guidance are highly important for us. However, they won't judge you on the practice delivery mechanisms in the setting, as it is more essential to demonstrate the impact you are having on your children.

You need to show that you are delivering a welcoming, nurturing and evolving practice which meets the needs and outcomes of all children who walk through your door. You need to grow as a setting and discover what works well for you and your children. You know your children better than anyone else. Remember that. You will have a range of techniques specifically suited to the learning styles of your children and you need to ensure that the quality of each endeavour with the children is of the highest form.

Think back... can you honestly say this is done consistently?

Again, to achieve the *outstanding* grading this needs to be done continually. You need to have achieved the whole of the good criteria in this judgement as well as the *outstanding* criteria. There is no best fit in the new Education Inspection Framework.

By meeting the needs of all the welfare requirements and the Statutory Framework for the Early Years Foundation Stage, you are well on your way of evidencing that you are meeting those needs. Once this has been achieved, you then need to look at your practice little by little to make sure this is effective for all children, and not just the ones who are exceeding.

What about children who need a little help, or the invisible child that doesn't give you a stressful day or the one who wanders around the room looking for things to do? The one who rarely engages in conversation with you unless you are asking a question... if that is the case, please make sure it's open-ended to extend their learning.

## The Dreaded Joint Observation

On the inspection day, the inspector will ask the manager to participate in a joint observation. The purpose of this is to gather evidence on how well the staff members are engaging with children, and how effectively the manager is able to evaluate the observation and make effective recommendations. It does not necessarily have to be the manager of the setting who takes part in the joint observation. In case, you have a teaching and learning member of staff who oversees the overall effectiveness of teaching and learning, they can also observe along with the inspector.

The observation does not necessarily have to be written alongside the inspector. However, it is recommended to make your own notes of your evaluations of the observation, to subsequently share with the team and identify the differences between the inspector and the observer. The inspector will want to see that you are observing what they are observing and a discussion will be undertaken regarding how to improve on the activity and the staff's interaction with the children.

Joint observations are not feasible with childminders who work alone. However, the inspector will want to observe individual children with the childminder and be able to discuss their learning progress/behaviour. At such times, you would want to make use of a volunteer to attend to your role.

This observation is a way of evaluating your practice. Here, one important point I want to draw your attention to is that please do not create an activity just for your inspector to see. This has happened many times during my inspections. Not only does it look false, but the fact is that children never lie, it creates a bad impression of fabricating false scenarios for inspection.

Some pointers when creating activities with children: My senior inspector taught me that everything I know as an inspector.

I need to think 'SO WHAT.' Think what is the INTENT, how am I going to IMPLEMENT this and what is the IMPACT.

So, with that in mind, attempt to adhere to the following guidelines.

Firstly, always engage in activities that would interest your children and this you would be able to identify by working closely with them, as mentioned before. Make a note of their interests as these are ever changing. Another exceptional way is to engage parents in these activities.

Why not send out this form out to parents every half term so you are able to work in collaboration with them? This shows an excellent working partnership as children's interests may be different at home to your setting and you will be able to bounce ideas off with each other.

With this collaborative approach, you are also able to choose which activity you wish the inspector to observe with yourself or with your nominated person. If you decide to decline the opportunity; for this to happen, the inspector must record this within her evidence. My recommendation is not to decline this offer. Instead, put this time to good use to showcase your connection with your children.

This is your time to shine and think about whether your decline would be a wasted opportunity to show what your setting does, how well your staff interacts with children, the benefits of such activities and the impact it has on the children's development and learning.

So, before the day of the inspection, make sure you have spoken to your staff about what is going to happen on the day and ask your staff if anyone wants to volunteer to be observed. This step not only ensures that all staff members are involved, but it also helps them feel valued and a part of the process.

Think about the types of activity you want the inspector to observe and the interactions staff members have with children.

**Quality of Education- Self Evaluation**

To ensure that you are ready for your inspection, why not start now in measuring how good your Quality of Education is. What is your intention, how are you going to implement and what is the IMPACT?

Take the time now before your inspection to address concerns you may have. Ensure that all team members are on board as this will show clarity and consistency when your inspection finally happens. Think about the quality of your staff interactions through their teaching.

Do they understand about sustained shared thinking and are able to question the children to perfect those critical thinking skills which are so important in the early stages of a child's life for their optimal development?

Through your own observations monitor the responses of children when being questioned and observe the activities in which they are participating.

- Are they encouraging curiosity?
- Are they thinking about investigating further?
- How is communication and language promoted throughout the activities?
- Are staff members making eye contact with children during these valuable conversations and making children feel valued?
- Are they building from children's knowledge, recalling from previous events and using different teaching methods to suit children's learning styles?

I have been to several inspections and observed what it takes to develop an understanding of the observation, assessment and planning cycle. You get this right from today and for the longer-term, it is sure to have an infinitely positive impact on children's outcomes and help them prepare better for school.

Use the form below to help you with your joint observations.

At the end of the joint observation, you and the inspector will discuss your collective findings. Just like with any reflections in your setting, it is imperative to understand your practice observations. They help you and the inspector (and your team) to gain an understanding of the development of your team. It will demonstrate your knowledge of how children are learning and developing and how you as a manager are aware of how to make progressive improvements.

The observations will be able to assess not only practitioners, but also the person who is observing alongside them. They will want to see a good evaluation and how this impacts children as well as the development of staff members.

If you are part of a childminding network, I would use this opportunity to carry out observations on each other, something similar to peer-review. This shows outstanding practice on how to improve on your own development in a practice where you are very much working on your own.

The Education Inspection handbook (2019) informs us that

*'The inspector should always invite the provider or a nominated senior member of staff – such as the manager or Early Years professional – to take part in one or more **joint observations** of activities, care routines and/or scrutiny of the progress children make. If the provider declines the opportunity to take part in joint observations, this should be recorded in the evidence base, along with the reason given.*

*Joint observations should enable the inspector to:*

- *Gain an insight into the effectiveness of the*

*provision's professional development programme
for practitioners*

- *Learn about the provider's view of staff's
interactions with children*
- *See the quality of the implementation of the
**curriculum**/educational programmes*
- *Consider how effectively the manager supports staff
to promote the learning and development of all
children.'*

If the quality of the practice shows differences and fails to meet the expected standards, it is important that the inspector talks to you about what was observed. The inspector will subsequently want to see how you plan to ensure improvements are being made and how these will be monitored.

You and the inspector will agree on a time to give feedback to the practitioner and manage the situation well. The inspector may seek involvement in this scenario, so they are able to see how you as the manager are performing this task. This is all part of the joint observation and will be recorded within the inspector evidence of the day.

Points to remember:

- Be prepared
- Ensure you are contributing to peer observations before the inspection, so it becomes a natural process within your day-to-day running
- Be evaluative. Understand what needs to improve and how you are going to achieve this.

| Room: | Date: |
|---|---|
| Observer 1 (name): | Observer 2 (name): |

Practitioner being observed:

Activity being observed:

What is the INTENT?

How is this IMPLEMENTED?

| Inside/outside | Number of children | Focused Activity | Area of provision | Snack or lunch time |
|---|---|---|---|---|
| (please circle) | | | | |

Observation:

Joint Observation Feedback

**Feedback notes from observers**

**Feedback from practitioners**

What is the IMPACT of the activity?

Actions Agreed and training required
*

*

*

Once you have started using the joint observation format, it will become easier and not come as a total shock when you are expected to do this with your inspector. By ensuring that you and your staff members are comfortable with this process, it becomes natural and this will have an impact on the outcome of your day.

## Cultural Capital

There has been much debate surrounding the words Cultural Capital and what it is supposed to mean. Basically, it is '*the essential knowledge that children need - to prepare them for their future success*'.

This is **<u>NOT</u>** another display board which you feel you need to place on the wall because OfSTED want to see. You need to be doing this, every day in your activities, on how well you are enhancing experiences for children and giving them more opportunities - particularly for the most disadvantaged children.

Each child is unique. We know that. Each child enters your setting with a range of experience that they have already received. However, the experiences and their range are unique to each child. As such, it is up to you to create positive experiences in children's learning and play and with the interactions from practitioners, which makes a difference for children. It is your job to create the awe and wonder of the world in which children live in, through all the seven areas of learning.

So, let me share with you some examples for better clarity.

If you are an Early Years setting which is based in a city, what do you give children to ensure they have the same experiences as children who live in the country.

For example, do children in your setting know about farm animals, the transport in farms, what young babies are from farm animals called, or where eggs and milk come from? It is your job to create those experiences in a setting which ensures that children are ready and prepared to go to school. They should have experienced a wide range of activities to impact a difference in their understanding of the world.

Take this time now to reflect on the experiences you provide for your children in your setting and how you enhance their learning for them.

Similarly, if you are an Early Years setting, which is based in the countryside, how do you ensure that children understand about the sea, about mammals and their young, about the plastic pollution of our oceans, about different tides and the textures and smells of seaweed and shells to provoke their senses. Where do fish come from, what do they feel like, how big can they get and what do they eat? This is just another example of how you can look at the experiences you are offering the children to provoke their curiosity and critical thinking.

Please remember this is just one example and you will need to reflect on the children that enter your setting to ensure what have experienced and how you can improve on these to ensure they are ready for their next stage of learning.

It is as simple as that!

Think

INTENT

IMPLEMENTATION

IMPACT

# BEHAVIOUR AND ATTITUDES

During the day of inspection, your inspector will make a judgement on children's behaviour and attitudes. This will be demonstrated through the characteristics of effective learning.

The aspects to these we all know is

- Play and Exploring
- Active Learning
- Creating and thinking critically

Another way of remembering these is

- Hand
- Heart
- Head

Without any of these being integrated within the day's

activities, there is no learning. Note, without your effective teaching children will not be learning successfully.

## The Characteristics of Effective Teaching

Inspectors will want to see the extent in which practitioners support children's' behaviours and attitudes, which does include how children manage their own behaviour.

Inspectors will want to see that children are able to have a sense of achievement of what they are developing in as well as a commitment to learning through the culture of your setting.

Think about how you do that in your setting.

Your inspector will want to see how you promote children's

physical and emotional health by monitoring their behaviour and conduct.

Think about how children are able to manage their own feelings as well as convey this to their peers and others. Another useful idea would be to discuss behaviour at a staff meeting in your setting and work out strategies within your team about how you can improve on this if you have any concerns. Document this as this will show you are being evaluative. Make sure you set a target date of when this needs to be achieved.

Did you know that your local authority will be able to help you with any concerns you may have regarding behaviour? Portage services look at working with families to help them develop and have life experiences for young children. They are able to support parents, settings, and children in minimising barriers that can threaten children and support the services that you can access. Ensuring that you are making accurate observations about children who have concerns with regarding behaviour is principal to ensuring that all outcomes for children are met. Your inspector will want to see what services you access and how this supports a child's development.

**Attendance**

Attendance also needs to be monitored in your setting as this not only ensures the safety of children, but also builds relationships with their own key person. Continuing attendance is extremely paramount to building relationships with staff and children's peers. The inspector will want to see how you monitor and record attendance. They will want to explore how you work with parents to promote children's attendance, this will help children with their future learning when they start school.

Be mindful that you ensure that attendance is being recorded effectively. When your inspector arrives, they may well check your register and count the children who are in the room. When was the last time you spot checked this?

Take some time to just count children in the room and see if they have been marked in on the register. This is highly important to make sure you and your staff register the time and sign in when a child enters and leaves your setting. You have a duty of care to protect children and this will help ensure you are monitoring this.

I say this as this has happened while I was inspecting. The register was not complete and at the time the kitchen had set off the fire alarm – luckily this was a false alarm. However, when children and staff arrived outside at their fire point they had more children than on their register. My point here is you need to accurately record how many children you have in your setting at any one time. This regulation is essential for protecting children and must be necessarily adhered to at all times.

Do you get parents to sign their children in with time and signature or do you rely on staff to do this?

Whatever way you record this - remember the word impact.

What is the point of you recording this? Remember duty of care as well. Regarding attendance records, do you record the time of arrival and departure of each child? If not, why not?

**Safety**

Exceptional practice in any setting - whether you are full day care or a childminder - is to be able to demonstrate that the need to ensure safety is paramount and high on the agenda of your setting. Recording the time of children arriving and departing with a signature highlight the duty of care you have to protect children. We all know that you have to maintain records regarding children for a certain number of years, but think about why we do this.

You have a duty to protect children and show how you are going to achieve this.

You will need to be aware of any patterns of absences that may be suggested to other wider safeguarding concerns. Your inspector will look at how well you work in partnership with parents to promote children's good attendance.

Other pieces of evidence also need to be considered during this area of the inspection in terms of how well your policies and procedures are known by practitioners and how these are evident within your setting.

Are you able to demonstrate this being cascaded to staff and are they aware of the implications in case of non-compliance?

**Behaviour and Attitudes**

Again, let us just reinforce that inspectors will need to be able to see that managers and practitioners are able to support children's behaviours and attitudes, including how the settings help children to manage their own feelings and behaviour and how they relate to other children.

In order to reach a judgement regarding this area, the inspector must be able to use their professional judgement to consider the ages, development, and stages of the children in your setting.

So, think about what you expect from a child in your setting when they are having an outburst. Think about their age and whether you are expecting too much from them to understand why they are not happy. Think about what you can put in place to encourage children to self-regulate.

Within the Statutory Framework for the Early Years Foundation Stage (2017), it is clearly documented,

3.52. 'Providers are responsible for managing children's behaviour in an appropriate way. Providers must not give corporal punishment to a child.'

Providers must take all reasonable steps to ensure that corporal punishment is not given by any person who cares for or is in regular contact with a child, or by any person living or working in the premises where care is provided.

Any Early Years provider who fails to meet these requirements commits an offence. Providers, including childminders, must keep a record of any occasion where physical intervention is used, and parents and/or carers must be informed on the same day, or as soon as reasonably practicable.

Writing a behaviour policy is one of the key points, in terms of ensuring consistency when relaying boundaries with children.

There has been much debate about the word behaviour and I have read many articles and attended several courses regarding how we need to encourage children to self- regulate. We can only do this if we as practitioners learn to co-regulate with children, and, in turn, help them become more resilient.

Think about strategies you have established to help children to learn to calm down. For example, making emotion tubes, using breathing techniques to stabilise their breathing rhythm which in turn creates a sense of calm. These are easy to make and when children are able to do this with you, they will then learn the purpose- remember the INTENT.

So, when writing such a policy, it needs to be made clear and concise for all staff members to follow. Be sure to include in your policy stipulations for inculcating in children self-regulation of their emotions and the reason and the different strategies employed. This will show the inspector you are fully aware of different stages of behaviour development and how you are able to engage all children with their self-regulation methods.

You need to ensure that the following points are covered.

- Children need to be able to access a caring, positive

atmosphere and demonstrate the ability to self-discipline. They need to be kept safe from both physical and emotional harm.

- The expectation of children's behaviour needs to be high in embracing honesty and the need for good manners.

- For children to be able to achieve this, there needs to be mutual respect between practitioners and children as well as between staff. The relationships which are maintained need to promote a positive environment and children must have a clear understanding of what is/is not acceptable behaviour.

- Practitioners need to work with parents or carers to help improve the behaviour of children and endeavour to offer a non- confrontational solution when conflicts arise between children and practitioners. This will be provided by inculcating positive attitudes, establishing courtesy towards each other as well as practitioners and reinforcing the importance of parents as role models through being approachable and caring.

- It is good practice for each setting to have a nominated person named within the policy so that practitioners can voice their concerns. Why not call this Regulation Champion?

*'Children socialise extremely well and have a wonderful time with their friends. They demonstrate an exemplary understanding of sharing. Children thrive on the attention and fun they have with the childminder. She has an*

*excellent understanding of their moods, feelings and individual personalities, enabling her to support their emotional development extremely successfully.'*

**Nicola Facey, Childminder with assistants, Andover**

*The childminder's home is exceptionally well prepared to help children develop their self- help skills. She has designed the play areas to support children extremely effectively. For example, the den with storybooks provides a communication-friendly space. The space under the table supports social skills and she provides small spaces for the children to be comfy and secure. This helps children to choose where they need to play to meet their own needs. Toddlers are learning the impact of their behaviour on others. For example, when children are playing on and near the slide they think about how to share the space safely. Children thoroughly enjoy their meals and have a very sociable time.*

**Lynda Hall, Childminder Tadley**

Your inspector will certainly want to see children behaving well. However, good behaviour does not mean that they all sit quietly on the table. We all know this is not possible and not a great way for children to learn and develop. They need to have the freedom to choose what they wish and be able to manage their own feelings with their peers.

We know that some children's behaviour can have a huge impact on our day itself; can you imagine how this impacts other children and also the child himself?

I have grown to love a challenge of identifying disruptive behaviour patterns within a setting and find out the root cause of why it is happening. Children's emotional well-being is paramount and holds the key to the success of learning and development.

I need you all to be aware when reading this that negative behaviour can be a display of unmet basic needs. Your practitioners will be the first to identify any adverse behaviour in the children, as they are their key person. Find out why the child is behaving this way and help find a solution. The child is a tiny acorn and will not turn into a proud oak tree without the support of watering and nurturing along its journey.

On occasions, some signs of undesirable behaviour may be a cause for concern and this is abuse (and I am not saying this is true in all cases, but any untoward behaviour must be documented and acknowledged). It is your duty of care and part of the reporting requirement for you to recognise signs of any significant changes of behaviour and record/report them, if necessary, following your local area guidance.

Another reason which may cause unwanted behaviour is that your expectations of what the child can do may be unrealistic (too high or too plain) for their age and stage of development. This is why it is extremely important for practitioners to have a sound knowledge of child development so as to ensure that their expectations are not wrong for the children in your setting.

Once practitioners have this knowledge, this expectation, it needs to be communicated in an appropriate and easily comprehensible way for the child to understand. It also needs to be consistent. Remember, Rome was not built in a day and a child has taken months to get to this stage of behaviour - so expecting them to change in a week is highly unreasonable. And having any unrealistic expectations of an overnight reform will only make you, your team and the children anxious. Ensure that you keep parents involved in the strategies you have chosen as your inspector will want to see and hear how effectively you involve all those who are needed to make sure that the children's needs are holistically met.

Think about the environment you have provided to the children.

Points which you may want to consider:

- Is the area too big for children?
- Is there any way you can create quiet spaces for children - if they need to self-regulate?
- Is there a mix of diverse children that causes the child to behave in this way?
- Can you create areas and group time which enables the child to learn and develop without becoming angry or anxious to prevent unwanted behaviour?
- Is the space in your setting too visually stimulating?

This is important and research evidences that the vast array of colours can over stimulate a child's brain and cause behavioural issues. Here, first, you should rule out any issues of safeguarding concerns and ensure that the environment is suitable for a child to learn. Now, the next step would be to identify whether a child needs any additional support through outside agencies. This can impact a child's behaviour as they are not able to comprehend how to calm themselves or communicate effectively. Think about whether a child is having a transition at home which may also have an impact on this; for example, a new baby, parents' divorce, limited language skills, or even the overuse of a digital source such as a tablet.

Once every avenue has been thoroughly investigated and researched, only then initiate implementing the self-regulation strategies for the child. Your inspector will want to see what strategies you have in place for any behavioural issues and how effectively this has helped the child. In addition, use this time to show your observations where you may be able to assess what triggers this unwanted behaviour. Make sure you evaluate this and ensure that you explain what you are doing next to help the child's behaviour.

How do you include parents/carers, outside agencies, key person and the child on an everyday basis? Your inspector may want to talk to the parents of children you have concerns with to see whether you are sharing this information and if they feel content with the strategies you have in place.

**Biting**

One common incident in an Early Years setting is biting. This can cause friction between parents and staff, the child who has been bitten and for the biter themselves. This can also quite often be a cause for an escalation or a complaint.

Think about whether you have instated a separate Biting Policy or if this is included in your Positive Behaviour Policy. Your inspector will want to see this policy to make sure that you are following the defined procedure. This is the purpose of your policies and procedures. What you write in this is what you need to follow!

Do remember that children bite for a reason. Again, you have to find out why. While you try to understand this behaviour, please note that children do not understand why they feel the need to bite. They do not understand how this can hurt others.

Biting is a form of exploration of their environment, especially with young children. Think about whether they are hungry and thirsty as this could perhaps be their way of communicating to you - as they are unable to relay this information any other way.

Some children bite because they are teething or because they want your attention. If this is the case, turn your attention to the child who has been bitten as they need it more at that time. Children who have communication and language difficulties sometimes bite to get themselves heard.

I know I hear you say they are certainly doing that. If this is happening, think about outside agencies that can help you with encouraging children to communicate such as visual cards or sign language. One setting I had visited in my travels had a 'time-out area', where children went to sit and 'calm down' when displaying unwanted behaviour.

It got to the point where children took themselves to this

place in order to calm down, a behaviour they learnt. Think about the impact this has on the child in this area. Is this really an appropriate strategy to use to help children to display positive behaviour! I am hoping you are saying it isn't!

**The word SORRY!**

There has been much debate about encouraging young children to say sorry. Commonly, it is believed, this could have the opposite effect of what you are trying to achieve (i.e., kindness) and will lead children to not developing a proper understanding and becoming less kind and caring.

This is hard as we are brought up in a nation of saying sorry for the simplest of things and it comes as easy as the drop of a hat. Think about it, as a nation do we say sorry for the slightest of things and is that only lip-service or do we really feel sorry?

In your setting, you will encounter many incidents involving a victim and an abuser. Try and encourage children to realise what they have done, when they have displayed this behaviour and how it makes the other child/person feel.

As a practitioner, talk to the child who is the victim and explain to them that you are sorry that another child has hurt them. This turns your attention away from the perpetrator and turns your focus to the other child. This will encourage children to develop empathy skills; eventually, the child will start to display how sorry they really are.

If this is the way you encourage children in your setting,

make sure you put this in your Positive Behaviour Policy and explain the reason to the inspector. They will want to know the impact of your decision in your setting. Again, the word IMPACT comes into play.

You need to provide clear guidance to your inspector on the children's understanding of 'What is acceptable behaviour'. And, if you have older children, for example, in an afterschool club, it is a good idea to encourage children to create their own behaviour contract.

I have seen this in several afterschool clubs. Not only does it give older children a sense of autonomy, but it also gives them a sense of self-worth that they are being listened to. When your inspector arrives in your afterschool setting, encourage children to interact with the inspector and explain about how they put the contract and rules together. This is highly effective and also covers British Values given that children have a voice and are able to give opinions.

Under this judgement the inspector will want to see if the children have high levels of respect for each other. And assess, if they are able to show they are confident learners and demonstrate the understanding for rules regarding behaviour.

**Patience and Independent Thinking**

Have you ever been in a setting where a child has explained to another child that they need to share and they are going to watch the sand timer – when it finally reaches the bottom of the glass then it is their turn. This is just perfect and would be ideal if we could encourage this in every setting.

The ideal scenario is when the children are able to make those right choices to enable learning to take place. Here, they demonstrate high self-control and when they are struggling they persevere. We step in far too quickly sometimes when they are struggling, especially if we are in a rush. Think about this when children are going outside, or getting ready for snack or lunch time. Try to stop and watch what happens when a child is trying to do up their zip, place their right feet into their wellington boots, wash their hands, and turning the tap on. These moments are just perfect to encourage independent skills and children should be able to take pride in what they have achieved.

Children need to be able to listen well and have high levels of concentration. They should be equipped with the necessary skills to use their curiosity to learn through their play. They should be able to listen to instructions and use these to become motivated learners who want to engage more. This enables children to become safe and secure in their surroundings.

If children's behaviour is poor within your setting this shows that learning will be poor. We need to be aware that if children are not engaged and actively involved in their activities, this can lead to poor behaviour. This, in turn, will hinder children's learning not only for themselves but for others. If this is the case, be mindful this would lead to an inadequate grade for the setting on inspection.

**Confidence**

We all know that children need to be able to be confident learners, be very self-aware and understand whether they are successful or not in their achievements of learning. Inspectors will want to see how children bounce back from their less-than-perfect results if needed, and how they are able to become resilient to adverse outcomes.

Through life's challenges, children need to be able to come back and thrive through the numerous strengths they have developed with the aid of their key person. We have an innate drive regarding the capacity of resilience; however, this does have to be worked upon not only in our lives but the lives of children.

We need to be able to encourage resilience with children as early as possible, be the role models that children desire us to be and ensure that we are building and encouraging children's confidence at all levels of their learning and development.

Your inspector will want to see that children are able to be independent and have the ability to explore, think for themselves by themselves and use their imagination. Using the basis of Characteristics of Effective Learning will help children prepare for their transitions within your own setting, whether this pertains from room to room or during the reception year at school.

In this section children need to be able to demonstrate their positive attitudes through their curiosity and their high levels of engagement as well as their resilience. They need to be able to listen and respond positively to you and each other.

*'Children thrive in this stimulating environment because of the excellent interactions they receive. They demonstrate*

*how they confidently manage their own feelings and behaviour. For example, children independently go and get the sand timer and say, 'I need this because I am struggling to wait my turn'.*

**Little Men and Misses, Northfield**

Children need to take pride in what they have achieved. Take a look at your children in your setting. Do they do this? How can you encourage more resilience and being proud of what they have achieved?

# PERSONAL DEVELOPMENT

The next reporting judgement is Personal Development.

Inspectors will evaluate the extent to which your setting is successfully promoting children's personal development. They will use their own professional judgement to consider how effective your setting is as regards the children's all-round development. They will ensure whether or not the setting is mindful of the ages and stages of development of each child.

Evidence of planning within the area of children's personal, social and emotional development will be used to see how you are able to supplement the inspector's observations.

The impact of their findings will secure your grading in this area and other pieces of evidence are likely to include:

- Evidence of how children's well-being is assessed.

- Discussions with key persons, children, and parents regarding the key person system and their effective use.
- What experiences children are being given to provide a sense of understanding surrounding our families, as well as communities different to our own.

Practitioners must be able to teach children how to express themselves and share their emotions in a way that is appropriate.

> 'The dedicated staff team focuses its energy on ensuring children are happy and secure in their environment. Staff support children's emotional well-being with expertise, ensuring their voices are heard and their interests are nurtured. Children display high levels of positive behaviour. They have an impeccably strong sense of belonging and are proud of their nursery'

**Starfish Day Nursery, Oldham**

Take the time to reflect upon this in your setting.

How do you ensure that children are confident enough to manage these transitions? Write down the transitions of your children with your staff team.

These transitions are accompanied by emotional security and attachments for the practitioners. Attachments with key persons need to be robust to ensure that children are confident within their own development and are ready to explore their new surroundings and environment.

Again, take the time to talk to your staff and ask them how extensively they know their key children.

This is so important.

Ask questions such as what the children's likes and dislikes are.

- What are they interested in at present and how is this being cultivated and developed?
- Are they able to autonomously evolve their self-learning?
- Do they have a schema and how is this knowledge being used to increase their life skills and improve on their own development?
- Do children feel safe with their peers and show mutual respect?

If questions like these are answered well, you can safely say that your key staff members know their key children and this earns them a substantial credit.

**Key Person**

Children succeed and thrive from a foundation of secure, warm, and loving care provided by the key people in their lives. During the day, we as practitioners become that person by taking on the role of the main carer - providing the stability, support, and comfort to the children. The key person is required to get to know the child's personality well so that they can understand and meet their specific needs.

An example of an outstanding report would read like this:

> *'Enthusiastic staff have an excellent knowledge of children's interests. They plan exceptionally well to ensure that children build on these through rich and varied activities that engage them and help them to be motivated to learn. For example, inquisitive children explore 'curiosity' cases. They select vintage or unusual objects that are unfamiliar to them. Children are incredibly confident to find out more or make suggestions about what these things are.'*

**Honeysuckle Day Nursery, Reading**

Think about how you choose the key person for a child.

- Do you wait until a child builds up relationships with an adult when they first start at the setting?
- Do you encourage home visits with an allocated key person, to arrange a meeting with the child alongside the parents and initiate to build on the attachment from the start?
- Or is the key person chosen because they only have seven key children and all the other staff members have eight?

Whichever way you choose the key person, pause and think about the impact this will have on the child. Why are you following this particular selection method and how can you improve? We know we can all improve, but ensuring that we are continually striving to develop our own skills will guarantee that we are a reflective setting.

With this in mind, do you have a Key Person Policy? Do all staff members know the reason they have been assigned the role of a key person, or is it something you always have done on an auto-mode?

Do you have a key person buddy system for when the key person is not in the setting? If so, brilliant, this shows you are ensuring children's needs are being met. If not, introduce this now to ensure your consistency in the quality of care in your setting.

Why not think about using one as part of your induction programme so that all staff members are aware of the underpinning reasons?

The key person must be able to provide the following for a child:

- Close attachment
- Familiarity
- Supported learning
- Comfort
- Encouragement
- Learning opportunities
- Consistent boundaries

Your inspector will want to see what support each key person gives their key children.

Things to remember:

- How many key children should be assigned to one key person, to effectively ensure a good partnership with each child?
- Does the key person support each of their key children to become familiar with the setting and to feel confident and safe within it?
- Is the key person the practitioner who provides maximally possible comfort and care for their key child?
- Does each key person develop a genuine bond with each child and their parents - supporting children to form secure relationships?

## Fundamental British Values

Under this area, children's personal development will be monitored, in the context of how well prepared they are as regards a wider society and life in Britain. This means that fundamental British values will need to be evidenced to show its impact on children.

This, however, does not mean a display board. This is not what your inspector wants to see. They will want to see how children are able to understand the fundamental rules within your setting.

Are they involved in making these rules?

I have seen many settings who are able to exemplify British values in their everyday practice and here are just some examples.

. . .

## Rule of Law

Children in an afterschool club are able to create their own rules. As an activity, they use this time to discuss what they want to follow in their setting and create a poster to remind all children that the rules were made by children for children. This activity evidenced an impact which was huge as it gave children the autonomy, self-confidence and self-worth in helping boost their self-esteem.

A preschool that I visited a few years ago used superhero characters as their rules. For example, at a child's height, they had placed several of these as reminders to themselves of what is right or wrong. Superman was used as a reminder to use their walking feet. Similarly, Snow White was a reminder to be polite by saying Please and Thank You, and Spiderman was used to portray to be kind with our hands.

I observed children reminding each other of these characters. For example, when running, one child pointed his friend to Superman and recapped the need to walk. This was a delight to see and is a great example of the rules made by children for children ethos.

## Mutual Respect and Tolerance

Mutual respect and tolerance for others is about learning to understand and appreciate each other's differences without allowing those differences to cause a change in the treatment of any sort. It is about being a cohesive part of a diverse community where not everyone is the same and forming relationships within that without discrimination.

Think about how you promote this conformity with diversity in your setting. Naturally, we are promoting inclusivity where we value different faiths and cultures, but how do we explore these fully, in order to ensure that we encourage children to recognise differences and similarities and exchange ideas irrespective of individual ethnicity.

Again, your inspector does not want to see the obligatory display board with people all around the world. Think about what impact this has on children's learning. Think about the everyday practice and how you encourage children to tolerate and thrive with each other. Children need to be given a wide range of opportunities to be able to practice tolerance and challenge any stereotypical behaviour they may occur. Children also need to be able to share ideas and stories that really value their diverse experiences and encourage them to learn from each other.

## Individual Liberty

In addition to being confident, through learning self-awareness, children need to have a positive sense of themselves. You can provide opportunities for children to develop this and increase their confidence in their own abilities. Enable children to have a voice and take risks, talk about their own experiences, explore own feelings, reflect on their differences and concurrently value other children's opinions.

Having the chance to share how they are feeling when they

are preparing for the transition to school is one observation, I was able to make in a pre-school I inspected. They used the small group time to prepare children for the next stage of their learning. Herein, they were able to listen and used the loose parts table for children to illustrate how they were feeling by looking in a mirror and creating their emotions on the wood slice.

Practitioners were able to talk to children about what they would be feeling when they started Year R. In fact, they refrained from calling it 'Big School' as they felt this would create anxiety among children. Instead, with the use of words with positive connotations, they wanted to encourage the children's confidence for the next stage of their lives. The impact was indeed thought provoking within this setting as children were given a voice and were being heard. They relished in their key person engaging in conversation with them, and you could see that children were very confident and excited about the next phase of their journey.

**Democracy**

As part of democracy in British Values, children need to be able to have a vote. This links to personal, social and emotional development; and the practitioners need to encourage children to know their own perspectives, value each other's views and make decisions as a collective force. An idea would be to encourage children to vote on which activity they liked best during the day. Children should be given adequate opportunities to develop their curious minds, in an environment where their questions are valued.

I believe that children's emotional well-being does affect

their behaviour and welfare. Get this right and certainly, children will be in the right place to learn effectively. This is so important. We sometimes forget that children have feelings and the things we do to ensure they are learning can be reduced to a tick box exercise.

To remember use this acronym

Democracy

Rule of Law

Individual Liberty

Mutual Respect and Tolerance

Take this time to reflect on your setting and think about the last time you just listened to a child's conversation, their worries and successes without recording it somewhere.

*'The stimulating environment helps children learn successfully. Staff value children's choices. For example, older children vote for their choice of storybook on arrival. Younger children show an exceptional understanding of routines, particularly lunchtime, which promotes high levels of independence. Staff are extremely encouraging about children's understanding of respect for others. Children thoroughly enjoy Spanish lessons that help them to use language that other children speak at home. Older children visit a local care home to learn about differences of age and to support their awareness of the community'*

**Honeysuckle Day Nursery, Reading**

**Keeping children Healthy**

Ask yourself and your staff on how they and the children keep themselves healthy. In fact, the topic constitutes an imperative agenda for the staff meeting exercise. As when asked this question by the inspector, practitioners can often freeze and struggle to explain themselves.

Part of the reporting requirements is to explain to your inspector about how you keep the children physically active. Do your staff members know how many minutes of the day children need to be active?

With 1 in 10 children not meeting the minimum required amount of being physically active each day, the Department of Health campaign aims for children to be moving and promoting physical activity for at least 180 minutes per day. This can be recognised as tummy play in the babies to being able to walk unaided as they grow from toddlers to children at the age of five as not sitting for long periods of time.

Many of the settings, where I have visited had taken away the chairs and used small quiet spaces for children to use when they needed to rest. This impact shows that children are active when they are standing at a table doing an activity. Take this time to reflect upon how much 'sitting down' a child does in your setting and how can you show that you are encouraging them to be physically active.

Think about the snack children are able to have.

Do children have a choice and is the choice wide-ranging?

Do you speak to children about healthy food and encourage this from an early age?

One setting I visited created a lovely activity at their 'coming together' time, which is widely referred to as the circle time.

Children were asked to sit down a circle and two trays and a basket of snacks were kept in the middle. I, along with the manager of the setting was observing this activity.

The purpose was - is the snack a want or a need?

Lots of thought-provoking questioning was used to extend children's understanding of why we need certain foods. Children delighted in sharing how it would make them big and strong. Practitioners explained the difference between a want and a need to the children.

Children encouraged each other and shared their points of view of about the want for a biscuit - but the need for a banana.

**Personal Self-Help Skills**

Encouraging children to be healthy is high on Ofsted agenda and you will need to be able to demonstrate this to your inspector. Think about how you support children to be independent throughout their time in your setting.

There are several ways to do this, from toilet habits to encouraging children to wash their hands to even the simplest of things such as blowing nose.

If you see a child who needs their nose wiped, what do you do?

- Do you get a tissue and wipe their nose for them?
- Do you ask them to find the tissue box and collect a tissue?
- Or do you have a nose blowing station where children are able to do this for themselves and see what they are doing?

I have seen this in several settings now and highly recommend it being placed in all rooms from the toddlers to preschool.

Nose Blowing Station: Set aside an area, where there is an acrylic mirror on the walk, with words to the effect of: Does your nose need blowing? The sign should be in bold print for children to see clearly. In addition, a mirror is placed on a table that has a box of tissues which are replenished as soon as they are finished, along with a bowl of soapy water and hand towels. Encourage children to look in the mirror and explain to them about keeping their noses clean and washing their hands after doing so. One setting I visited were concerned that children would use the same water to wash their hands. I would recommend changing the water every few hours, but nowhere in the Statutory framework is this stated as an unhealthy practise.

*Children acquire a strong sense of emotional well-being.*
*They are great risk assessors and show self-control in a*

*range of situations. For example, when being 'builders' children are aware of the need to wear safety goggles. Children have access to a wealth of interesting and innovative resources and play experiences that greatly support their interests. For example, children use magnets to investigate which objects are metal and they share their findings with others. Children relish their time as the 'responsible' helper. They confidently take orders from their friends and help to serve them healthy snacks.*

**Compton and Shawford Preschool**

This is an excellent way of encouraging children to be independent with their self-help skills.

Within this section of the Personal development as practitioners we need to 'help children to gain an effective understanding of when they may be at risk, including when using the internet, digital technology and social media and where to get support if they need it'

Children should be made aware that they need to keep themselves safe. How do you ensure this awareness as well as the implementation of this safety?

There has been much discussion regarding the number of times children are engaged in screen time. If children are unable to access the internet in your setting think about how you help parents understand the importance of their children using the internet. We need to be raising awareness of how important it is to know what children are looking at when they are online.

We need to be giving clear consistent messages to children that support healthy choices around their health and wellbeing.

Through conversation or encouraging the children to talk about the risks within the setting? Another outstanding example is encouraging children to risk assess themselves with their own risk assessment sheets, which they create themselves. By provoking an engaging conversation about whether something is safe or not can help a child to think this on an everyday basis.

Encourage the responsible helper to use their own forms, where they are able to mark the score using a tick sheet or tally the resources and activities. Not only does this give a child a sense of pride and well-being, but it also gives them the power to use and apply their brains for risk, prevention, and correction which in turn helps them in making decisions and being resilient.

> *'Staff observe children's emotional behaviour when outdoors and understand the importance for children who need to be physically active. As a result, the pre-school children enjoy challenging themselves outside as they use natural resources, such as large tree stumps, to develop their physical skills.'*

**Melton Day Nursery, Woodbridge Suffolk**

You must also make sure that you have the following as part of the welfare requirements

'Where food and snacks and drinks are provided they must be healthy, balanced and nutritious' – How do you ensure what you provide comprises of all these things?

Think about children's lunchboxes: How do you ensure these are healthy?

The time to actually talk about what is expected from parents is when they visit with their child at the very beginning, especially regards the lunch boxes. Talk about how there may be allergies within the setting and you need to make sure that children are kept safe from any unwanted goodies (which is a want, not a need) such as crisps, chocolate, and sweets.

Fresh drinking water must be available at all times – How do you do this? Please be mindful that if children have their own water bottles, they only access this as opposed to just taking any random bottle at any time. Stomach bugs can spread all too quickly and the children need to be monitored constantly to prevent any such infection.

There must be an area which is adequately equipped to provide healthy snacks and drinks. Include suitable hygienic preparation of food and drink for children.

How do you ensure that the areas where you prepare bottles and food are constantly cleaned? Do you document this?

For this safety, just a handful of the welfare requirements need to be abided by, to ensure a risk-free environment. See the Statutory requirements of the Early Years Foundation Stage for the full version.

**Diversity**

Think about how you ensure that children know about similarities and differences between themselves and others and among families, faiths, communities, cultures, and traditions?

When I asked these questions during my Quality Improvement visits as well as Early Years inspections, I often heard the reply, 'Well, we have a Polish little boy and we ask his parents for words to help him understand and we invite them in to talk to the children.' Another classic example is, 'We celebrate Chinese New Year and do a Food Tasting.'

No disrespect to these activities, which you are providing for the children, but think about when a child leaves your setting. What cultures are they able to see and relate with, in the outside world? Are they able to identify any other cultures or faiths? Ensure that you are able to demonstrate to your inspector that you encourage children to be aware of the cultures and faiths outside their own. This all comes under the umbrella of mutual respect and tolerance and should be demonstrated in your setting.

Consider the kind of impact this has on children's lives and how we can start encouraging children to be asking questions about how other people live from all around the world.

Think about your INTENT, IMPLEMENTATION, AND IMPACT!

**Welfare**

How are the children keeping themselves safe? Does this include their safety against the abuse of the internet and social media?

This may not be suitable for your Early Years setting, but if you are a childminder or afterschool club, how do you ensure children are keeping themselves safe? Also, what documentation and safety measures do you have in place to protect the children?

Overall quality and effectiveness of your provision

Your inspector will want to be able to evaluate your quality, and it is up to you to ensure that they are able to see this by being consistent, transparent and clear in your delivering of Early Years.

Specifically, the inspectors will evaluate and report on:

- How well your setting meets the needs of the range of children who attend.
- How well practitioners know their key children and where they are in their learning from their starting points to the next stage of their education.
- How well is the curriculum (EYFS) planned, designed and implemented.
- The contribution of your setting to children's well-being and whether they are emotionally safe, secure and happy.
- The effectiveness of leadership and management of

your setting especially in the evaluation on how to improve.

So remember,

- What is your INTENT?
- How are you going to IMPLEMENT this?
- What is the IMPACT?

# LEADERSHIP AND MANAGEMENT

Leadership and management assume great importance in the Early Years settings. To be a good leader, you need to shine from the top and ensure your team is aligned with you to take the journey with you.

*'We must be the change we wish to see in the world.'*

**Mahatma Gandhi**

Without your team being a part of your ethos, you will struggle to achieve as much as you want to. The inspector will want to assess and evaluate the effectiveness of your leadership and management in terms of subsequent impacts on your setting. This chapter will break down the areas that must be demonstrated/described and give examples of what you can showcase.

## Judgement of Leadership and Management

There are several questions that you need to ask yourself so that you are confident in your answers.

These answers will facilitate the judgement of leadership and management by evaluating the level of the following:

- How do you demonstrate the vision of your setting? Do you have high expectations of what the children in your setting can achieve and ensure that you have corresponding high standards of care for the children?
- How do you improve your staff's practice of teaching and learning and provide effective levels of supervisions so as to ensure that you are promoting appropriate professionalism?
- How do you evaluate the quality of your setting and ensure that the accounts of the staff, children, and parents are taken into consideration to ensure progressive improvement?
- How do you implement learning programmes and a curriculum that meets the relevant statutory requirements during the Early Years Foundation stage, whilst also considering and addressing the issues relevant to the children's interests?
- How do you successfully plan and manage the curriculum/learning programmes so that children get a good start in their learning journey and are well prepared for the next stage of their learning as well as the bigger picture before being ready for school?

- How do you record the IMPACT of what you implement?
- How do you constantly promote equality and diversity ensuring that British values are demonstrated and that poor behaviour towards others is acted upon? Here, the term poor behaviour needs to include bullying and discrimination. The required learning outcomes of different groups of children also need to be demonstrated and accordingly met.
- How do you make sure that you meet all the statutory and other government requirements regarding the protection of children, promoting their welfare and are alongside able to prevent radicalisation and extremism?
- How do you ensure that all children, irrespective of their background are ready for their next stage of learning? How do you ensure that each child experiences the awe and wonder of the world and is ably equipped to apply those experiences to prepare them for school?

Considering the following guidelines, we will break down each section, specify what this means and how you can ensure that you are meeting the needs of the requirements with impact.

### Safeguarding

One of the reporting criteria at which an inspector will take a close look is: 'How effective is your safeguarding within your setting?' The aim is to ensure a thriving and safe and secure environment for the children in your setting. They will consider how well the leaders and managers have created a culture of vigilance where children's welfare is accorded the top priority. In addition, they will also evaluate in case there are any concerns and that these are acted upon swiftly.

Safeguarding covers a huge spectrum of parameters, which not only come under the Leadership and Management area but also includes personal development. So, if you have a safeguarding concern at your inspection, please be aware that this will impact both judgements in these areas.

Settings will need to consider the Working together to Safeguard children (2018) and Information sharing for practitioners (2018); in this reference, please note the date as the new versions should be used. In addition to these, Prevent Duty also need to be digested and used within your own safeguarding policy.

Please also consider the 'Inspecting safeguarding in Early Years, education and skills settings' Ofsted 2019. This guidance gives you the core information regarding the expected range of evidence required by an inspector on the inspection day. This guidance should be read in the context of the Early Years Inspection Handbook 2019.

**Five Main Aspects of Safeguarding**

The inspectors investigate five main aspects under the safeguarding remit. These include:

- How leaders, managers, and providers (this

includes a committee) ensure a positive culture and ethos, to ensure these become an important part of everyday life within a setting. This also includes all levels of training in safeguarding, at every level.

- The effectiveness of the safeguarding policies includes safer recruitment and vetting processes. In addition, the staff should be able to recognise and identify the signs when children may be at harm either within the setting or in the family or wider community outside the setting.
- The quality of the safeguarding practice should entail the functionality that staff is aware of the types and signs of abuse whilst ensuring that the welfare of all children is kept at the forefront.
- The response time, if any safeguarding concerns are raised, should also be factored in devising the safeguarding framework. This is so important and often compliant visits are raised because concerns were not actioned quick enough or directed to the right organisation.
- The quality of support when working with multi-agencies around a plan for a child.

Inspectors will need to consider how you, in the capacity of a leader or manager has instated the following arrangements under the listed headings:

**IDENTIFY** children who may need any early help or are at risk of neglect, abuse, grooming, and exploitation.

**HELP** prevent abuse by raising awareness among children

of any safeguarding risks and who and where to get help in order to support them when needed.

**HELP** those children who are at risk of abuse and need Early Years help or statutory social care involvement, keeping accurate records, and ensuring timely referrals. In addition, it is essential to have working liaisons with other agencies to ensure that children get the help and support they need.

Also, to be able to **MANAGE** allegations about adults who may be a risk, and check the suitability of staff who work with children.

We will cover each section and explain what needs to be evidenced throughout the course of your practice.

Firstly, how does the committee, leader or yourself, if a childminder, ensure a safeguarding culture and ethos is promoted through everyday practice.

Inspectors will want to see the following:

- Policies that have been reviewed regularly and demonstrate the incorporation of new legislation/documentation: Have they been updated with the new Working together to safeguard children (2018) Please ensure you check this.
- Staff members are supported to develop an awareness of signs that a child may have been neglected or abused and have knowledge of 'What to do if you're worried a child is being abused'
- All staff members, leaders, committee members and

volunteers must receive appropriate safeguarding training, which needs to be updated regularly. It is pertinent that all are aware of their responsibilities regarding how to protect children from harm.

There needs to be a Designated Safeguarding Lead (DSL) in charge of safeguarding with the appropriate level of training who fully understands that it is their responsibility to ensure all children are kept safe and that all staff members are up to date with their training and remain confident in the knowledge to recognise any concerns.

The Statutory Framework for the Early Years Foundation Stage effective from 3rd April 2017 states under Section 3:

*3.2. 'Providers must take all necessary steps to keep children safe and well. The requirements in this section explain what Early Years providers must do to: safeguard children; ensure the suitability of adults who have contact with children; promote good health; manage behaviour; and maintain records, policies and procedures.'*

As well as:

*3.5. 'A practitioner must be designated to take lead responsibility for safeguarding children in every setting.*

***Childminders must take the lead responsibility themselves.*** *The lead practitioner is responsible for liaising with local statutory children's services agencies, and with the LSCB. They must provide support, advice, and guidance to any other staff on an ongoing basis, and on any specific safeguarding issue as* *required. The lead practitioner must attend a child protection training course that enables them to identify, understand and respond appropriately to signs of possible abuse and neglect'*

Operating in the capacity of a childminder, you are the DSL and hence, must take on the responsibility yourself. You need to ensure that your training is suitable to meet the needs of the safeguarding of children in your setting.

The inspector will want to speak to the DSL to ensure that the Lead is confident in the referral process of any safeguarding concerns. When asked questions, the designated personnel should know the process confidently, be thorough in their knowledge of the setting's safeguarding policy and ensure that they give the inspector enough confidence that they know the mandated procedure in case of any untoward incidents.

In case any referrals have been made, the inspector will want to check whether this was shared with the local authority, in conjunction with timely written secured records. You do have 48 hours to share the information, but as a qualified safeguarding instructor, I can say that it is paramount to get those forms to the correct agency as quickly as possible. Your policy also needs to state the time limit within which you need to have all the documentation sent to the correct agencies.

Your inspector will also check for any safeguarding incidents or allegations, since the last inspection and whether these have been resolved or are ongoing. These will, in all probability, be checked as early in the inspection as possible as it will impact your judgement as regards your effectiveness of safeguarding.

Settings must also be risk assessed and this needs to be demonstrated to your inspector. You have to protect babies and children and to ensure that age-appropriate, reasonable risks form an adequate part of their development.

When it comes to safeguarding children, the Framework (2017) confirms:

*4. 'Providers must have and implement a policy and procedures to safeguard children.'*

This policy will be asked for during your inspection, including several others. These will be checked and clarified to ensure your compliance and adherence with what is stated in your policy. If you are not following your own policy, this could, in fact, lead to an inadequate grading.

Regarding Child Protection, the framework affirms the following:

*'These should be in line with the guidance and procedures of the relevant Local Safeguarding Children Board (LSCB). The safeguarding policy and procedures must include an explanation of the action to be taken when there are safeguarding concerns about a child and in the event of an allegation being made against a member of staff, and cover the use of mobile phones and cameras in the setting.'*

You will also be aware about smart devises which staff are now wearing. Is it appropriate for staff to wear these, do they need to and what procedures to you have in place to protect children from the use of them?

Have you considered these in your policies?

If not please ensure you do. A smart watch will have a lens to take pictures and these are easily able to download from.

So, for example, a staff member could position their phone somewhere with a clear view of the nappy changing area and remotely access the phones camera on their smart watch from somewhere else in or outside the nursery. They would have the ability to zoom in using the smart watch and take multiple photos.

This will be something inspectors will be checking for in your policies as a line of enquiry. If staff are wearing these devices, what protection do you have in your setting for children. Make this an action to check today.

Please be mindful that as per the Working together to Safeguard Children (2018) the Local Safeguarding Children Board will be transitioning to new multi-agency arrangements led by the three safeguarding partners (i.e., the local authority, clinical commissioning groups, and the chief officer of the police).

Your policy MUST follow your Local Safeguarding Children's Board procedure to report any concerns as well as an allegation against a member of your staff. It is also recommended to allocate a time frame to do this, in case you have a concern or a disclosure.

This is important, and inspectors will want to know that your

Designated Safeguarding Lead is fully aware of what to do in case of unforeseen scenarios.

When writing your safeguarding policy, you will realise that it is extensive in terms of the influence. Here is a list of subheadings, which need to be covered. Remember, this needs to be bespoke to your setting.

a) List the types of safeguarding concerns that may arise in your setting.
b) How should you deal with these concerns?
c) What is the timeframe within which these concerns are to be informed to relevant authorities?
d) Who is the designated safeguarding lead?
e) Details of recruitment and supervision of staff (this does include your assistants if you are a childminder).
f) How you create a safe environment?
g) How you record and store information in line with GDPR?
h) How you will respond to any complaints or allegations against staff?
i) Details of Prevent duty and FGM.
j) What are the regulations concerning the use of mobile phones and cameras?
k) What are the protocols for E-safety?

This list is not exhaustive but it does give you a fair idea on what to include.

**Prevent Duty and Potential Questions**

The inspector will also focus on understanding and assessing the knowledge level of the staff regarding Prevent Duty and FGM.

As an ex-inspector, there were questions which I needed to ask and record as pieces of evidence to ensure that the staff members were aware of how to recognise any signs and report the same to the DSL.

Examples of potential questions include:

1. What does the Prevent Duty protect children from?

2. How would a childcare setting demonstrate that they are protecting children from being drawn into terrorism?

3. In what existing policies would you expect to read about the Prevent Duty?

4. If you suspected a child was being radicalised, to whom/which authorities would you report your concerns?

5. What signs would you look out for if you suspected a child was being radicalised?

6. Can you name all of the British Values that should be embedded into your practice and how do embed these into your everyday practice?

**Vetting Process**

The staff as well as volunteers need to be carefully selected when joining your setting and should be vetted in accordance with the statutory requirements. This should be reflected in the protocols defined in your application and recruitment procedure. The inspector will also speak to staff in your setting to ensure that the stated procedure is being followed. Usually, conversations are initiated with the newest member of your team.

If you have assistants as a childminder, it is also important for you to show that they applied for the post using the defined channels and highlight the steps taken by you to ensure their suitability. This needs to be recorded as a process and for a demonstration to your inspector.

## Working in Partnership

*'TEAM WORK*

*Coming together is a beginning*

*Keeping together is progress*

*'Working together is success'.*

**Henry Ford**

Working together in partnership with others is very high on the agenda during your inspection. How do you ensure that all parents feel they are being valued; they are interacting and engaging with their children's development and that you are listening to their voice? Also, how do you work with outside agencies to ensure that children's needs are being met?

The Early Years Foundation Stage (2017) states:

*'The EYFS seeks to provide **partnership working** between practitioners and with parents and/or carers.'*

If you can honestly say that you have all parents on board in your setting and that you are consistently working together to improve outcomes for children, this chapter is not for you.

However, I truly feel that we, as child educators need to ensure we are engaging with all parents and carers and have strategies in place to make this happen.

Examples of the efficacy with which partnership is shown in an Ofsted report might look like this:

*"The childminder enthusiastically works with parents and shares ideas for home learning through home link books and activities. This actively encourages an excellent partnership with parents. She is excellent at communicating information with parents regarding their children's care, learning, and development.'*

**Nicola Facey, Childminder**

*'Partnerships with parents are excellent. Information sharing between staff and parents is highly effective. The parent's involvement in their child's learning ensures that children's needs are quickly identified and successfully met. Highly active links with the local schools and other settings create a tremendous sense of belonging for children and their families.'*

**Shawford and Compton Preschool, Winchester**

*'The nursery uses a panel of professional people, including parent representatives, to conduct interviews with any new staff members to ensure the best person is*

*employed for the position. In addition, there are very comprehensive, safer recruitment processes, before and during employment, which are regularly reviewed and constantly improved.'*

**Melton Day Nursery, Woodbridge Suffolk**

These settings showed how their partnership with the parents was outstanding. They all knew their parents' needs and styles, which allowed them to help build the foundations of partnership. Parents' involvement was developed through a variety of methods in order to make it highly effective. They included the parents in the whole process of recruitment, thereby ensuring collaboration at its best.

Right from the time when a child first starts at your setting, you should inform parents of who their key person is. This is mandatory. The Statutory Framework of the Early Years Foundation (2017) states:

*1.1 'Providers must inform parents and/or carers of the name of the key person, and explain their role when a child starts attending a setting.'*

Think about what you do in your setting.

- Do you wait for a child to be given a key person?
- What makes you decide on the key person?
- As per the regulations, it is a 'must'.

Children need to build attachments to their key person who will subsequently ensure they are forming safe and secure relationships with their key child. In turn, this will give them the basis to know this child well enough and be ready to develop their learning through the environment.

*2.1. 'Assessment plays an important part in helping parents, carers, and practitioners to recognise children's progress, understand their needs, and to plan activities and support.'*

How do you do this? Try answering the following questions:

- What method do you use to observe, assess and plan for a child? How do you ensure parents are involved in this process?
- Do you use an online tracking tool and give parents the login to see where their child is in the development cycle?
- How do you ensure parents understand how this works?
- Why not invite parents to an evening's training about how the online tool works and use this time to emphasize the importance of working in tandem whilst assessing their children?

I understand that it can be a time issue, with parents being so busy, but there is nothing worse than having this as a recommendation in your report when, in fact, something could be done about it.

Do your parents know that this is a reporting requirement and would affect your judgement grade? If not, LET them know.

I am sure if they knew they would do everything they could

to help you gain the rightful judgement during your inspection.

The new Education Inspection framework (Sept 2019 page 41) states:

*'Leaders engage effectively with children, their parents and others in their community, including schools and other local services.'*

I have inspected many settings. In my experience, when managers are asked the question about how they work in partnership with parents, they say they do their best to encourage this, but not all parents want to be involved in these conversations.

Firstly, when I would hear this, I would think that you are giving yourself a recommendation for your own report. So, before you start answering this question, think about all the ways in which you encourage parents to share their children's learning development. Please do not focus on parents who don't - think positively about all the parents who do focus and engage.

With this in mind, at Jigsaw Early Years Consultancy Ltd we have now created online training called 'The Parent Bundle'. So the purpose of this is to encourage and settings to engage with all parents. As we can appreciate, time plays a huge part in working together. We have created a package, which you can purchase for parents when they start with you at your setting.

This bundle has four online lessons which they can use on

their own devices. Also, there are fact sheets and guidance on what to expect when their child starts at your setting. What better way to engage with those hard-to-reach parents and feel you are working together in partnership! This mechanism can have a huge impact on the way children learn and develop. If this is something which interests you to ensure engagement of all your parents, please email us on info@jigsaweyc.com with the subject of 'THE PARENT BUNDLE'.

Another question you may like to ask yourself: How do you work with other settings? Again, this is a reporting requirement and hence, will certainly be asked. It will also be followed up with seeking clarification from different staff members.

Think about how you do this? Do you send emails? Do you make phone calls? Do you share learning journals via your online tracking system? These channels adopted by you – do they work, is this two-way, interactive communication? If this does not work, why not?

What is your intention to improve on the communication between you and the other settings? How are you going to implement this and what is the subsequent impact on children's learning and development? Do you have any recorded evidence of this?

**3 I's Formula**

**Consider this:**

**INTENT**

## IMPLEMENTATION

## IMPACT

What better than to use the 3 I's formula to demonstrate how you are evaluating your setting?

Going back to partnership with others, another 'faux pas' is to tell the inspector that you have tried to contact the other preschool, childminder, nursery but FAILED to get any response.

Do you recognise that in your setting? Have you tried all the possible strategies to engage with other settings? Can you honestly say that you have exhausted all options?

If you are not receiving any responses from other settings, why not give them a call and be honest with them. Explain that one of the reporting requirements within the statutory framework is to work with other settings and share development, strategies and needs of the child. Explain that as part of this process, you would like to work with them and explore the possibility of sending end-of-term reports to each other that can be used as a piece of evidence to show the inspector.

I cannot stress enough how important it is for settings to work together. In addition to being a good and outstanding practice, it shows you are according top priority to the child's needs.

So, think about outside agencies, and try and identify the agencies, using the following question: Do you know who you can work with and how to find out if you are able to receive help? This can be a mind-boggling question.

In many leadership and management discussions, the majority of managers and childminders, when asked this question, would say the same thing:

*'We have tried to contact agencies but with limited funding, they are not able to help us'.*

Sadly, we all know children's needs have to be met, however, we attribute our failure to the funding crisis. And this, in fact, may not be the case.

With the closure of children centres and the cutting off of your local council's funding, you may not be able to access the support you need. For example, for a child with behavioural concerns, do you have a Portage Service which can come out and support you? If the answer is no, have you thought about contacting The Local Health Visitor as they may have a direct line, or may be able to help you by visiting and giving you some new strategies?

If you have concerns about a child's communication skills, are you able to contact the speech and language therapist of your local children's services and ask for some help? Quite often, the answer is 'there's a waiting list.' In such cases, my advice would be not to delay in sourcing help. I am sure you will have kept records of observations, so when they do hopefully visit, they would be able to see that you have tried everything in your capacity to help that child to secure the required support. Again, please make sure parents are kept in the loop of association with other agencies.

There has to be a way of receiving additional help if needed and you as the settings leader or manager will need to find that way. Remember: Children's needs must come first.

## Questions to Consider When Working in Partnership

How do you ensure that your parents are happy? Such questions should start to provoke your thinking about what you do with your current set of parents? And, what is it that you can do to be in sync with the parents' understanding of happiness.

Do you use questionnaires and if yes, how often do you send these out?

What do you do with that information and do you inform parents about the answers to the questions as a summary of your findings?

By doing so, you would help parents feel they are being listened to and are active participants in the development of their child. So when asked by your inspector whether their views are taken into consideration, their answer would be a confident YES.

What about a comment box? Do you use any such form or tool for encouraging parents to place their comments? How often do you look inside this box! Do remember that there is no point in providing a suggestion/comment box if you are not willing to act on the comments shared in the box. Also, you may be pleasantly surprised with some of these comments being positive feedback! How great would that be to share with your team, letting them know they feel valued?

Think about this:

Do you consider the views of outside agencies? Think about the ways you gather and collate information from outside agencies. Do you have a good rapport with them and how do you ensure congruity between your/their thought process whilst taking them seriously? This again assumes great importance for working with partners.

Do you record these details and again what do you do with this information and how do you show their impact on your setting?

Remember though that when you are sharing information with outside agencies, parents need to sign their consent, clarifying their agreement with this. This needs to be collected at the very outset when the children start with you.

Consider when they do not agree to sign the form. Do they have a valid reason for this? In case, parents do not agree to give their consent on the information sharing form, this also needs to be recorded.

Is this a cause for concern? And what are you going to do with this information?

Parents and carers need to be aware that if you have concerns about the well-being of their children, this becomes a 'duty of care' and you need to report this immediately regardless of whether they have signed the consent or not.

How well do you work with others to help you understand a child's development and ascertain ways of improving their learning? Think of the way you work with other settings' childminders, preschools or nurseries to develop better insight on a child's development. How do you record this and show its impact on the child and your setting? Do you share children's Progress Check at 2 with the Health visitor or do you only give a copy to parents? Think about if parents do not pass a copy of this very important document to the Health Visitor. With the absence of this information, some key points and concerns may not be communicated effectively. So my advice would be to share this with the Health Visitor as part of your ongoing working in partnership with outside agencies.

Have you considered encouraging parents to complete questionnaires to help you evaluate your practice? If not, why not?

**Example of a Questionnaire**

Dear Parents,

As part of our self-evaluation, we are constantly striving to improve upon our practice and would appreciate your willingness to share your views on this. All answers will be treated anonymously.

Please put a cross in the box as your answer.

We will collate the information and send out the report to you summarising our findings and any actions that are needed.

Scale:

Strongly Agree = 4

Agree = 3

Disagree = 2

Strongly disagree = 1

| Statement | 4 | 3 | 2 | 1 |
|---|---|---|---|---|
| The induction procedure helped my child to settle nicely within the setting. | | | | |
| My child is happy to come to the setting. | | | | |
| My child feels safe at the setting. | | | | |
| My child is making good progress within his/her room. | | | | |
| We are aware of his/her next steps of learning. | | | | |
| We feel we are adequately involved with his/her care and education in the setting. | | | | |
| We know who our child's key person is. | | | | |
| We feel we can talk to the key person regarding our child's learning. | | | | |
| We are kept well informed about our child's learning and receive termly reports. | | | | |
| Our child's behaviour is being managed effectively. | | | | |
| The setting helps our child feel confident. | | | | |
| The learning experiences acquired by our child at the setting are at the appropriate level for them. | | | | |
| Our child is encouraged to be healthy and physically active. | | | | |
| The setting gives us ideas on how to support our child's learning at home. | | | | |
| Our child was duly supported when they started in the setting before moving to a new room. | | | | |
| All staff members are approachable, and we feel that we can freely ask them any questions. | | | | |
| Any further comments | | | | |
| Date: | | | | |

Thank you for taking the time to complete this questionnaire.

This is just an example and the wording may need to be amended to suit the needs of your setting.

Examples of Questions from The Ofsted Inspector for Parents

The Ofsted inspector may want to speak to a parent about the questionnaire and possibly ask a couple of questions to see how happy they are with your setting.

Examples of these inspector questions may include:

1. How long has your child been at the setting?

2. How often do they come to the setting?

3. What made you choose this setting for your child?

4. What was the initial, settling-in procedure like for you and your child?

5. Do you know where policies are kept and have you received a copy of the same?

6. Do you know who your child's key person is?

7. How often do you discuss your child's development?

8. What information is passed on during the pick-up times?

9. Do you know who to approach if you have any concerns?

10. In case, you have any concerns about the manager or owner, who would you go to?

11. Did you know Ofsted has a complaint number you can call? The inspector will always direct parents to the Ofsted complaint number which needs to be displayed on the parents' notice board.

12. Would you recommend the setting to others and why? In terms of achieving an outstanding, it is a good practice to ask parents questions about your setting especially because they are also your partners.

So why not give them a questionnaire to complete on a regular basis. This will not only make them feel valued but will also help iron out any concerns which may arise and allow communication to run effectively.

This will not only ensure achieving an outstanding practise, but also the parents would be prepared for the questions on the day of inspection. Again, these questionnaires can be answered anonymously.

In addition to questionnaires for parents, why not give your staff time to answer a version also.

Example of A Staff Questionnaire

Dear Staff Member,

As part of our self-evaluation, we are constantly striving to improve upon our practice and would appreciate your willingness to share your views on this. All answers will be treated anonymously. Please place a cross in the box as you answer each question.

We will collate the information and send out the report to you summarising our findings and any actions that are needed.

Scale:

Strongly Agree = 4

Agree = 3

Disagree = 2

Strongly disagree = 1

Statement 4 3 2 1

| Statement | 4 | 3 | 2 | 1 |
|---|---|---|---|---|
| I find it rewarding to be a member of the team in this setting. | | | | |
| I feel a valued part of the setting's community. | | | | |
| I am encouraged to learn and share practices with my colleagues within my setting. | | | | |
| I am given the chance to share best practices with colleagues from other settings. | | | | |
| I have a clear understanding of the vision of the setting. | | | | |
| I am supported to engage in professional learning. | | | | |
| Staff members treat each other with respect. | | | | |
| Staff members treat children with respect. | | | | |
| Children are encouraged to treat each other with respect. | | | | |
| Parents and staff treat each other with respect. | | | | |
| Staff members are aware of how to encourage children to self-regulate. | | | | |
| Staff members at all levels communicate effectively with each other. | | | | |
| Staff members effectively engage all parents in their child's learning. | | | | |
| The setting is well-led and managed. | | | | |
| All children are engaged in their learning. | | | | |
| Children are provided with experiences which meet their learning and development needs. | | | | |
| Children are involved in the planning of their learning process. | | | | |
| I receive support for my development. | | | | |
| I am listened to regarding my emotional mental health and well-being. | | | | |
| I am listened to regarding my work load. | | | | |
| I am listened to if I want to make changes to the way my room is run. | | | | |
| I am actively involved in the setting's self-evaluation. | | | | |
| I understand the settings procedure relating to safeguarding and child protection. | | | | |
| Any other comments<br><br><br>Date: | | | | |

Building on from working in partnership with parents and staff and using the questionnaires to summarise your findings, consider doing the same for working in partnership with other settings. This also can be done anonymously, either by (i) sending out forms to the settings you work with or by (ii) creating a Google form where you can send the link and the responses will come through.

Examples of Partnership Questions

1. How long have you been working in partnership with the setting?

2. Do we work in partnership on a regular basis?

3. Do you feel you are being listened to?

4. Do you know our safeguarding policy and procedure?

5. How does your setting provide relevant information about the needs of the children?

6. Does our setting value the contribution made by your organisation?

7. Does the setting share best practices and networking with others?

8. How does the setting work overall in partnership with yourselves?

## Policies and Procedures

A policy needs to ensure that it covers the beliefs and values of your setting and shows how you deliver best practice, including Early Years care and education. These are standards that can suitably guide you to be able to demonstrate a professional approach and continually deliver best practice.

They need to be easily comprehended by all staff members, parents, and carers. Your policies will inform your procedures and minimise risk for both children and staff within your setting. Your procedures take shape from your policies and specifically pertain to a series of actions which are carried out in a particular order.

Not only staff members, but parents and carers also need to know about the nuances of your policies and procedures. This is not a pointless exercise merely to show off to the inspector during the inspection. Policies and procedures protect you, your setting and most importantly the children.

Inspectors will need to consider a sample of policies and these will include safeguarding and child protection, risk assessments, fire safety and any other policy that relates to health and safety, like the medicine policy and behaviour management policy.

The Statutory Framework of the Early Years Foundation Stage (2017) states:

*'3.3. Schools are not required to have separate policies to cover EYFS requirements provided the requirements are already met through an existing policy.*

Where providers other than childminders are required to have policies and procedures as specified below, these policies and procedures should be recorded in writing.

***Childminders are not required to have written policies and***

*procedures.* *However, they must be able to explain their policies and procedures to parents, carers, and others (for example Ofsted inspectors or the childminder agency with which they are registered) and ensure any assistants follow them.'*

A practice which achieves good to outstanding shows that childminders are fully aware of their policies and that these are documented, well-maintained in their folder or digitally and are bespoke to the childminder. I have been to many settings, including childminders, where they have thought it would be a better option to 'buy' the pre-written policies from the many sites.

Firstly, ask yourself this…Why?

Is it to save you the effort of writing them yourself? If so, when you use them, do you even understand what they mean? Consider if the wordings need to be customised and changed to make them right for you and your practice.

This is your setting, so make sure your policies are aligned to you and not written by or for anybody else. This not only helps you when you get inspected, as you can always refer to the policies written by you; it also helps you take ownership of your setting.

There is nothing worse for an inspector to see these pre-written policies with no changes to show that you haven't reflected upon each and taken ownership. You are only drawing negative attention to yourself, which will entail further questioning and investigation about what you know about your setting.

One of the most important policies will be your safeguarding policy and this will certainly be asked for during your inspection.

## Health

The Statutory Framework of the Early Years Foundation Stage (2017) states:

*'3.45. 'Providers must have and implement a policy and procedures for administering medicines. It must include systems for obtaining information about a child's needs for medicines, and for keeping this information up-to-date. Training must be provided for staff where the administration of medicine requires medical or technical knowledge. Prescription medicines must not be administered unless they have been prescribed for a child by a doctor, dentist, nurse or pharmacist (medicines containing aspirin should only be given if prescribed by a doctor).'*

Think about how you ensure that staff and parents are kept informed of your policies and procedures; when do you do this; and how often do you review your policies?

## Complaints

The Statutory Framework of the Early Years Foundation Stage (2017) states:

*3.74. 'Providers must put in place a written procedure for dealing with concerns and complaints from parents and/or carers, and must keep a written record of any complaints, and their outcome. Childminders are not required to have a written procedure for handling complaints, but they must keep a record of any complaints they receive and their outcome. All providers must investigate written complaints relating to their fulfilment of the EYFS requirements and notify complainants of the outcome of the investigation within 28 days of having received the complaint. The record of complaints must be made available to Ofsted or the relevant childminder agency on request.'*

Your inspector will want to check your complaints folder to ensure that all complaints have been recorded and processed for resolution. Any complaint needs to be reported to Ofsted for maintaining necessary records, regardless of how small it is. I cannot emphasise this point enough – doing so will help you show how professional you are in following your own policy to the inspector.

## Policy Sharing

Firstly, staff should be aware of your policies through the robust processes implemented by you in the setting. For more information, read the earlier paragraph within this chapter. You need to ensure that staff members are kept up to date with any amendments being made to your policies.

As a previous group manager, in my personal experience, it was extremely difficult to guarantee that ALL staff members were aware and updated of these changes. One idea we had as an outstanding setting was that we used to place a new policy on the back of the toilet door. Staff informed us that this was a good way of reading the policies and even though this seemed odd, it worked!

Staff meetings were also another way of making sure that

every member was kept up to date and also, the policies were signed by the staff to certify that they understood the new changes. This is also a good way of sharing good practice and ensuring that all staff members understand the changes and their implementation.

So contemplate, how do you make sure ALL staff members are aware of these changes if they do not attend staff meetings? Again, this is something that an inspector will ask the staff during the day of inspection.

## Writing Policies

It is an excellent idea to get your entire staff involved in writing your policies and serves as an additional mechanism to evaluate and embed your practice with current policies. This should not only include staff but also your committee members if you have a committee run pre-school.

During my time in Early Years, I have written more policies than I care to mention. I always dreaded the time when a new version or new legislation came into play, and I had to write yet another one adding to the vast 50 we had!

As time progressed, it became easier, with the use of a structured format. The list is immense and here are a few examples:

- Accident and Incident Policy
- Admissions Policy
- Behaviour Policy
- Biting Policy
- Compliment and Complaints Policy

- Equal Opportunities Policy
- Healthy Eating Policy
- Lost or Missing Child Policy
- Non-Collection of Child Policy
- Risk Assessment Policy
- Safeguarding Children Policy
- Settling-in Policy
- Trip Policy
- Whistleblowing Policy

These documents are very important as they will help you run your setting effectively and show to the inspector you have a good understanding of your business operations. Again, make sure they are unique to your setting.

**Training and Qualifications**

The inspector will want to check the details of the training attended by you and your staff and also the associated IMPACT (there is that word again!) it has had on your setting and the children.

We know training staff can be a problematic issue, particularly with lack of money, time out of the setting and finding the right course to meet the needs of staff members. You should be able to have documented records about the needs of your staff through the instated supervision and appraisal process. Their use can help you find the right course and at the time of inspection provide evidence that you are trying to upskill your workforce in order to make a difference within your setting.

The training stipulates also apply to the childminder and

their assistants. As their manager, you need to show the inspector that you value each of your team as an employee and are actively encouraging new knowledge and skills in your setting.

The Statutory Framework for Early Years Foundation Stage (2017) states:

**Staff Qualifications, Training, Support and Skills**

*3.20. 'The daily experience of children in Early Years settings and the overall quality of provision depends on all practitioners having appropriate qualifications, training, skills and knowledge and a clear understanding of their roles and responsibilities.*

*Providers must ensure that all staff receive induction training to help them understand their roles and responsibilities. Induction training must include information about emergency evacuation procedures, safeguarding, child protection, and health and safety issues.'*

*'Providers must support staff to undertake appropriate training and professional development opportunities to ensure they offer quality learning and development experiences for children that continually improves.'*

*'Childminders are accountable for the quality of the work of any assistants, and must be satisfied that assistants are competent in the areas of work they undertake.'*

This reporting requirement and documentation is needed to demonstrate that your staff members are constantly improving on their skills.

The question that arises is: How do you do that?

## Professional Development Questions

Part of the inspection process will pertain to assessing the impact training has had on your setting, staff and children.

Inspectors will want to see the staff's continuous professional development folder and ask the following questions:

- What was the last training that was attended, and what you did when you returned to the settings?
- Did you do anything with the new information you were given?
- Do staff members complete a training evaluation sheet and share with the rest of your staff?
- Do you share information at your staff meeting so that everyone who was unable to attend can get an insight into what was learned?

What is the point of this, I hear you say?

Firstly, think about how each staff member has their own learning journey, just like your children. You observe, assess, and plan for children. Here's something that must be carefully noted: Training is exactly the same for staff members.

- You observe staff in your setting on a day-to-day level
- You assess where they are in their understanding

- You plan to help them improve, and hence the new training

Remember that training is not just a tick box exercise. You need to ensure knowledge enrichment and improvement, and this is not only through face-to-face training. Several other ways can be utilised to achieve knowledge development:

- Reading a book
- E-learning
- Reading blogs or journals
- Attending other settings and sharing best practice

One thing which needs to be reiterated is that we also can improve upon our practice.

Think back to this: Do you ever get days where you observe your staff and think that they have lost their way a bit? They seem to have lost their mojo, which is impacting the delivery of children's learning?

Have you ever felt that way for yourself?

Ask yourself this: When was the last time you had **FIRE IN YOUR BELLY?**

Collins Dictionary states that 'If you say that someone has fire in their belly, you are expressing approval of them because they are energetic, enthusiastic, and have very strong feelings.'

- When was the last time you had those feelings?

- What made you feel energetic and excited to share, learn and influence more?
- Do you still have those feelings? If not, why not?
- What do you feel you need to get it back again? Is it motivation? Is it time? Is it training?
- Or is it all of the above?

Training and continuous development is another non-negotiable reporting requirement. Inspectors need to explore how you are ensuring the staff's upskilling and consistent improvement.

> *'The childminder continually strives for improvement and attends many relevant and childcare courses to further develop her already excellent skills. For example, following a course in the different ways children learn, she implemented specific resources to support children's individual learning styles even further.'*

**Maimuna Khan, Childminder, Southampton**

The findings of the Nutbrown Review in 2012 helped with the understanding of how important upskilling and our continual professional development. It stated:

*Good quality CPD enables existing practitioners to build on their knowledge and skills and to keep up to date with relevant research, practices and initiatives, including learning from examples in other countries. Practitioners who undertake regular CPD show a proper respect for the children and families they work with, taking a professional pride in their work and demonstrating an understanding of their responsibility to constantly improve their practice and enhance the experience they are able to offer young children.*

This is extremely important in Early Years, our staff, parents, committee members, as well as our inspector, are continually told that we are a workforce that needs to be valued, nurtured, and trained.

One of the findings of the Nutbrown review was that over half of the settings stated that the range and qualifications of the training did not meet the needs of their staff. Specifically, 72% identified that the cost of training and covering staff members attending the training put a huge strain on their financial status, which prevented the staff from attending this course.

Nutbrown (2012) emphasised the importance of accessing courses by the settings to grow their workforce and also stressed this should be evidenced during the Ofsted inspection.

Thinking back to the chapter on self-evaluation, remember:

WHAT

SO WHAT

NOW, WHAT?

What was the point of the training?

Are you able to demonstrate the evidence of the impact of training on you and your setting? If yes, how are you able to show this?

## Qualifications

A couple of years ago, the Department for Education (2014) stated that staff who were level 3 qualified after 2014 needed to have Maths and English GCSE graded C or above so as to be included in the ratio. This guideline significantly impacted the numbers of Early Years educators who entered the workforce. College numbers decreased due to the only selective enrolment of students in the course based on their relevant GCSEs. The recruitment crisis was so overwhelming that it affected a major dent on the college classes and enrolment.

From April 2017, specific changes were incorporated in the new inspection framework. The changes were attributed to the consultation results stating that staff qualifying at level 3 Early Years Educator with any suitable English and Maths qualifications, in addition to functional skills as well as GCSEs should be included while computing the staff: child ratios. The Government's decision to reinstate functional skills is now encouraging recruitment in colleges as well as apprenticeships.

Your inspector will want to see copies of your staff's qualification and will record this as part of their evidence for your report.

## Ratios

According to the EYFS (2017), for children aged below the age of two:

- There must be at least 1 member of staff for every 3 children.
- At least 1 member of staff must hold a full and relevant level 3 qualification and must be <u>suitably experienced in working with children under two years of age</u> (think how you can demonstrate this- training, past employment.
- At least half of all other staff must hold a full and relevant level 2 qualification.
- At least half of all staff must have received training that specifically addresses the care of babies.
- Specific to children under two-years-old, any member of staff assigned to their room must, as per the judgement of the provider, have suitable experience of working with children below the age of two.

This will need to be evidenced in the report that your inspector is writing while they are at your setting.

For children aged two:

- There must be at least 1 staff member for every 4 children.
- At least 1 staff member must hold a full and relevant level 3 qualification.
- At least half of all other staff members must hold a full and relevant level 2 qualification.
- For children aged three and above, in registered Early Years provision where a person with Qualified Teacher Status, Early Years Professional Status,

Early Years Teacher Status or another suitable level 6 qualification is working directly with the children,

- There must be at least one staff member for every 13 children.
- At least one other staff member must hold a full and relevant level 3 qualification.

For children aged three and above at any time, in registered Early Years provision when a person with Qualified Teacher Status, Early Years Professional Status, Early Years Teacher Status or another suitable level 6 qualification is not working directly with the children,

- There must be at least 1 staff member for every 8 children.
- At least 1 staff member must hold a full and relevant level 3 qualification.
- At least half of all other staff members must hold a full and relevant level 2 qualification.

Only staff members aged 17 or above may be included in the computation of the ratios. As such, it becomes necessary to know the following:

- Do you have volunteers in your setting?
- Do you know if you can include them in your ratios?

Students who are on long term placements and volunteers (aged 17 or above) and apprentices (aged 16 or above) working towards a qualification may be included in the ratios as long as you are satisfied that they are competent and responsible.

You must be able to ensure that this guideline is adhered to while computing the ratios and appropriately demonstrated.

**First Aid**

Much ambiguity seems to exist when it comes to First Aid and the use of such training in settings. This section will give you further clarity into the necessary requisites to ensure you meet the needs of the Statutory Framework.

To be compliant with Ofsted Statutory Framework for Early Years Foundation Stage (EYFS 2017) requirements, your staff should have a requisite number of members trained on First Aid from appropriate recognisable organisations, approved by HSE and Ofsted.

The training should cover the following:

1. Training needs to be designed for workers caring for young children in the absence of their parents and is appropriate for the age of the children being cared for.
2. Following training, an assessment of competence needs to lead to an award of a certificate.
3. This certificate must be renewed every three years.

With regard to the EYFS and Ofsted requirements, you should at least have one 12-hour full paediatric first aid qualified staff member available including medical cover for sickness, holidays, and trips. The 12-hour paediatric first aid trained staff can be supported by One Day Emergency Paediatric First Aid trained staff.

This requirement must be revisited and renewed every three years. Ensure that if your staff members and children are going on trips, one staff member must be first aid trained and carrying a first aid kit when they are out with the children. In addition, during any excursion, you will need to consider the number of children, staff, and layout of your setting to ensure that a paediatric first aider is able to respond to emergencies expeditiously.

All newly qualified staff to the Early Years workforce who have completed a level 2 and/or level 3 qualification on or after 30 June 2016, MUST also have either a full PFA or an emergency PFA certificate within three months of commencing work in order to be included in the required staff: child ratios at level 2 or level 3 in an Early Years setting.

Your inspector will check this ratio on the day of inspection and would want to see those certificates, which ideally should be on display or made available to parents, if needed. Please be mindful that if you have these on display and in accordance with the GDPR regulations you should have the necessary staff permission to display anything resulting in complete exposure of their names.

As evidenced in this chapter, training, and qualification is highly important to ensure that you are delivering high-quality learning to children and it has a positive and long-lasting IMPACT on their development. One thing to remember is to reflect on your learning process and think about how it is likely to impact your role as a teacher – today as well as in the future. While there is no one-size-fits-all recommendation, no matter where you are in your career or learning, these pointers will hold you in good stead and play a constructive role in helping you attain outstanding.

## Example Training Evaluation Form

| What did I attend and when? |
| --- |
| 'In The Moment Planning'<br>June 2018 |
| **Why did I attend the course?** |
| The setting wants to implement a new way of planning through encouraging and promoting ideas and interest from children. |
| **What did I learn?** |
| I learnt that we need to be focusing not only on teaching, but also on how well we know our children, the optimal use of our environment, and the questioning techniques we use as practitioners. |
| **How am I going to implement this into my setting?** |
| Through our staff team meetings, I will deliver an 'In The Moment' planning question and answer session. I will use the staff's knowledge and expertise to better understand children's interests. Concurrently, I will ensure we work with parents in order to understand a better way of informing about children's ever-changing development. |
| **How will I know what IMPACT it has had on my setting?** |
| Children's learning will be at the forefront of our planning and all the assessments will be ongoing. Staff members will have a deeper understanding of what the children's next steps are and thus, will not have to keep revisiting the tapestry. Children's assessment and planning will be at the heart of the setting and we will be able to produce evidence of what we are doing to meet the needs of individual children. |

Throughout the whole leadership and management chapter, you will have realised that evaluating your practice is of high priority. Ensure this approach is constant and integrated with the processes, as this constitutes a part of your own reflection of your setting as well as practice.

During the inspection process, you will also be expected to engage in a leadership and management discussion with the inspector. With this in mind, we have created a list of questions, which may help you ensure you are fully aware and completed prepared for this time.

1. How do you make sure the staff are gaining more knowledge and improving their skills?

2. How often do you conduct supervisions and appraisals?

3. How do the staff get involved with these processes?

4. What is the induction process for your staff?

5. What is your DBS process?

6. How do you cascade information to the staff?

7. What do you understand about Prevent Duty?

8. If I was to ask a member of staff about prevent duty would they know what it meant? (The inspector will also speak to staff member).

9. If you had concerns who would you speak with?

10. What does your staff know about British Values and how are these incorporated and applied in the setting?

11. How do you ensure you are listening to staff regarding the work load and their well-being issues?

12. Who is the Lead Safeguarding officer?

## Supporting Staff Wellbeing Issues

This is a new addition to the Education Inspection Framework (2019) and you will have to prove and maybe evidence how you consistently support your staff with their well-being issues. When delivering training for the new framework, this, in fact, emerged as the most debated topic.

Providers, leaders, and managers have raised their eyebrows and sighed. The reason being, they feel that they listen to staff regarding their well-being and needs; and this is another tick box exercise. It is noted that when staff and the team are happy and contented within the setting, staff are more likely to perform better. Thereby, adding impact to children's lives and helping them achieve more success in the setting. Moreover, work-related stress has a huge impact on our own performance and our own well-being, as well as those who we are working with i.e. children.

Use this time to get you and your staff in the right mind-set of being honest and map ideas on how you can improve on your well-being. Do this now. During your regular staff meeting ensure that each month you take 10 minutes to focus on how you can improve this within your setting. This would then automatically reflect in your minutes and your inspector will be able to see this is raised at every opportunity to support the staff who needs it.

Now you may ask who is there to support you if you are the

owner/leader or manager. Think about this for a minute or two and focus on when the last time you took a break – just for 30 minutes to give yourself some time to reboot. I know this is hard, as I always used to eat my lunch if I had any, of course, at my desk while I was answering emails and writing on the computer.

This is not good for our minds or our well-being and I cannot stress enough about taking a break. Schedule one break in your diary and stick to that time for de-stressing yourself. Once you start doing this you will find your performance at work will become higher and more achievable as you will be able to focus on some breathable time.

Within Jigsaw Accredited Online Are you ready for your inspection Kate Moxley who is a Mental Health First Aider has created a well-being toolkit for you to download and use. If this is something you would like more information about please email info@jigsaweyc.com

# SO NOW WHAT?

So, you have taken the time to read the book, dived into each chapter to explore what you need to do to be prepared for your inspection. And, what do you do next?

I am hoping you will have made notes along the way as an 'Action Plan' of what you are planning to improve upon. This is an excellent way of reflecting on your practice, as well as showcasing your evaluation process to the inspector, as this is still a reporting requirement. I am hoping you can now see how important your INTENT, IMPLEMENTATION, AND IMPACT is on the day-to-day running of your setting.

Since our last edition of this book, we are delighted that our #JustQuality ADDING IMPACT accreditation is now seeing outstanding results. It took us over six months to devise a programme, which not only helps you to evaluate where you are in your setting but also helps you to showcase the associated impact. This accreditation could not have come at a better time with the new framework starting in September. It is all about IMPACT!

We are also delighted the #JustQuality accreditation has now been recognised for a Nursery World award for staff resources and equipment.

We have settings that are embarking on the #JustQuality journey and have been receiving amazing comments from inspectors. This is not to say that it is only the accreditation that has achieved these results. It is the staff's motivation and constant reflection on what they need to improve upon that has enabled them to achieve the most prestigious of grades.

'The inspirational manager is dedicated to her role and makes a significant impact to drive forward improvement. Since the last inspection, proactive staff have positively reflected on all aspects of practice and the environment to enhance outcomes for children'

**Honeysuckle Day Nursery, Reading**

'Meticulous self-evaluation and reflection ensure the staff identify areas for improvement throughout the nursery exceptionally well. Leaders demonstrate an unswerving determination to remove barriers to learning and provide children with the very best of outcomes.'

**Starfish Day Nursery, Oldham**

There may still be times when you are thinking about what

else can I do? I need an outsider to come in with a fresh pair of eyes to see it for themselves.

This is exactly where Jigsaw Early Years Consultancy Ltd comes to your aid.

You have read the background and the WHY of us at the very beginning of this book. If this is something you feel you may benefit from then give us a ring, or write to us or feel free to drop in a message.

Our website is www.jigsawearlyyearsconsultancy.com
Our Facebook page is:
https://www.facebook.com/JigsawEYC/
Facebook group: Ask to join JigsawEYC
Facebook group: Ask to join Are you ready for your inspection?

# TESTIMONIALS

I thought I would leave you with a few testimonials from settings who have used our Quality Improvement Inspections as part of their evaluation.

*Dear Vanessa,*

*Thank you very much for your visit to our nursery for a Quality Improvement Inspection. As a twice 'Outstanding' nursery, who work incredibly hard to maintain that standard all of the time, we really wanted to be ready, to be confident and as well prepared for our big day as we could be to put us in the best possible position to maintain our grading, so felt that a QII would be exactly what we needed. You were recommended to us by a trusted colleague, and now we recommend you in turn.*

*Your visit was inspiring; you were professional and courteous, thorough and that filled us with confidence in your feedback. Staff were given valuable experience of inspection and were left feeling more confident, and even excited for their opportunity to shine. Your manager's interview and paperwork review were thorough and found a few issues that we have been able to rectify before they cost us our Outstanding, which was exactly what we wanted.*

*We have already booked you to come and give our new nursery a QII, as well as some consultancy on how to develop that new team, and I am excited and confident about our future, knowing that I have your input and support behind me and my team.*

*Thank you very very much again for such a positive experience.*

*With kindest regards,*

**Charlotte de Lacey**

**The de Lacey Montessori School & The de Lacey Day Nursery School.**

*Background to visit. After a very disappointing Ofsted visit, the Early Years at our school needed a thorough rethink. I was made Early Years Lead in February and began to analyse how the department could be improved. My own personal remit was to make it an 'outstanding' provider.*

*I had already started to implement changes but the enormity of what I had taken on was beginning to become apparent. Endless nights of trawling through Government requirements, joining chat groups for Early Years practitioners, visiting other providers.......I needed help, support and guidance.*

*Late one night I came across a competition for a QII and entered. Blow me down, a week later I received an email to explain that I had won! I never win anything. Thinking this could possibly be some kind of hoax, I phoned Vanessa at Jigsaw Consultancy. It wasn't a hoax. She really wanted to help. Vanessa listened to the background of the setting and wanted as much information as possible before her visit.*

*On the day of the visit, Vanessa arrived and immediately I could see her quietly assessing every aspect of the department. She spoke to staff in what appeared to be a very informal manner, but she was consistently acquiring an overview of the areas that needed to be addressed. As we talked throughout the morning I made notes of her recommendations (5 pages!). However, at the end of our meeting, Vanessa bought up every single point I had noted and also made more suggestions.*

*I had been 'Jigsawed'! I had a list the length of my arm. However, Vanessa followed up her visit with friendly emails to ensure that I was dealing with issues in a systematic and achievable way.*

*I have recently written a list of changes that have been implemented following her visit and I could now see that the department had changed and was moving forward in the right direction. There is still a lot more work to do, but Vanessa helped to shape these changes in a manageable way.*

*We are due a monitoring visit from Ofsted and also Vanessa is coming back to help some more! I will update you on the future outcomes for our Early Years Department.*

*P.S. Vanessa is now known as my Fairy Godmother*

**So here's the update I promised!**

*Since the beginning of May, I have been waking up every morning thinking 'today's the day'. The six months from our inspection had passed. The changes needed to meet standards had been met or were being addressed. We were ready for a visit. I truly wanted it to happen before the Summer holidays, so the team could have a well-earned rest.*

*Vanessa came back on Monday 2nd July 2018. She was blown away by the changes that had taken place. The setting was vibrant, energetic and full of happy children and staff. She agreed that we were ready for a visitor from HMI. There were 3 days left until the end-of-term. Surely they wouldn't come now?*

*Wednesday 3rd July.....................All the children were registered and had begun their last full day of planned learning. I looked at the clock, 9:35 am. I had lost hope that we'd be inspected before the summer break.*

*Then the Deputy Head popped her head into the room and looked at me with huge eyes, "Ofsted are here!" Behind me was a scene of devastation. The children had had a lot of fun that morning.*

*My TA and I looked at each other. Without saying a word to each other we knew what to do! Carry on and just do what we would normally do. I asked the children to put their wiggly fingers to work and tidy up. It was as if they could tell that they needed to do their best. Each child went off and completed a little task. One little boy looked at me and said "We're doing a good job just for you". (A goose bump moment mixed with a slight feeling nausea)*

*As the inspector arrived in the Early Years block I was in the middle of my phonics session. The children were on form! We had laughing and the children knew all their first three sets of sounds.*

*Somehow during all of this I had managed to find the time to phone Vanessa. The inspector wanted to speak to her too!*

*I was asked to attend an interview at 12:30pm with the inspector. It was a grilling, but I survived with support from my Deputy and Head also present. I started waffling about my passion for the department. Then verbal diarrhoea kicked in! He wanted me to supply him with some pieces of evidence to back up my claims. I ran off and returned them to him. He was on his own in the office. He thanked me and said with a wry smile "I think what I'm seeing here is rather good".*

*At the end of the day the Head called us all together and said that although she was not legally able to divulge the outcome of the inspection she wanted us all to go home and have a well-earned rest with maybe a few glasses of bubbles.*

*Now the long wait over the summer holidays for the report and findings to be audited. Watch this space for the next update. Another HUGE thank you to Vanessa. We couldn't have got to this point without your help.*

**Early Years setting, West Sussex**

*First of all, sorry for the long post - but it's the truth (I haven't been bribed into anything – it's from the heart)*

*I can't recommend Jigsaw Training enough. I do owe a lot to Vanessa. Thanks to her awesome training and signposting I managed to achieve "Outstanding" in my inspection last week. I was really craving an outstanding grade this time, as previously had 2 "Good" inspections.*

*The first training I attended was "Safeguarding" run on a Saturday. It was affordable and location was perfect. Having enjoyed the training and the way Vanessa makes quite serious topics interesting and engaging - I booked onto another training session in Gosport for Characteristics of Effective Learning, British Values, and Everyday Maths. CoEL and British Values were topics I just couldn't get my head around. Having attended the training all was crystal clear and I implemented these "new found" topics into my practice. It was at this particular training that something stuck with me. The talk was about having a "Good" grade and how far and wide this grade can be but why not aim for an "outstanding". Those words just stuck with me. Why not???*

*Another training I attended was a Webinar on "Are you*

*ready?" - this was also very helpful when I had the call from the inspector. I remained calm and asked all the questions I wanted to prior to her arriving. I would recommend this particular training especially if you are due an inspection, all you really need is covered within this topic.*

*No doubt I have booked onto Autumn training too which the OI was happy to see in my CPD folder.*

*Its affordable, informative, fun and full of passion - not a moment to be bored whether it be something important like Safeguarding or something fun like Everyday Maths.*

*Thanks #jigsawconsultancy #awesometraining #youarethesource #SoWhat*

**Maimuna Khan, childminder, Hampshire**

*Vanessa spent a full day at our nursery and I can honestly say it was the most interesting, beneficial experience we have ever had. Vanessa has to be one of the most knowledgeable and experienced professionals within the Early Years sector I have ever met. She simply oozes with passion and to quote Vanessa herself, she very definitely has 'fire in her belly' for everything Early Years.*

*We gained so much from Vanessa's visit, she gave us lots of useful pointers and ideas to enable us to further improve some areas of our practice. Most importantly for us though, she boosted our confidence in the work that we have been doing surrounding loose parts and evolving our learning environments to continue to inspire our children's natural curiosity.*

*Thank you so much, Vanessa, spending a day in your company was for all of us truly inspiring.*

**Jane Broughton, Manager of Tinkerbells Bridge inn Day Nursery, Preston, Lancashire**

*Finding #justquality was like finding the missing piece in our jigsaw (no pun intended)*

*It epitomised everything I was looking for in an accreditation and has really helped us as a setting value the difference we make in children's lives and has really helped us drive our setting forward. It has helped the whole of my staff teams realise the WHY we do things and just how much impact even the smallest things have on our settings ethos, and more importantly our children, families and staff team!*

**Chloe Heath Edwards, Owner of 3 nurseries Little Men and Misses Nursery**

*'I had been looking for a 'consultant' to come in and evaluate the performance of my staff and the environment of my setting. I felt that my staff were not performing as well as they have done in the past. I wanted to find a way of improving performance and practise overall and get the setting back on track to aim for OUTSTANDING. But it needed to be from someone who had 'authority' and for my staff to hear it from someone other than me.*

*I decided to sign up to the '#Just Quality ADDING IMPACT' award. It appealed to me as it's a journey for the whole setting to embark upon, to reflect on 'quality' and adding IMPACT – being a recognised accreditation was a Bonus.*

*However, before starting the accreditation, I felt it prudent to have an 'unannounced' Quality Improvement Inspection by Vanessa Dooley, Jigsaw Early Years Consultancy. Vanessa had been highly recommended to me by a fellow Day Nursery Owner who had also had a very effective QII from Vanessa and was also working towards the accreditation. Whilst there are other 'consultants' out there, I felt Vanessa's Ofsted Inspector training, knowledge, background & experience would be beneficial.*

*On 3rd July 2019 – Vanessa conducted an announced QII. Her findings (as detailed in the QII Report which she provides after inspecting) were shocking and disappointing – however, this was the 'wake up call' that was very much needed!!! I was actually pleased that Vanessa's was able to identify and highlight areas of underperformance and how our biggest resource 'The Staff' were missing opportunities to provide quality teaching and learning opportunities to the children. Vanessa has an in-depth knowledge of Tapestry (which we use) and was therefore able to identify that our current 'tracking of children's progress' was ineffective. She conducted observations with my Manager who was shocked by some of the Staff's missed opportunities and immediately realised things needed to change too.*

*We held a staff training meeting with Vanessa at the end of the day (after the QII) to discuss the QII Report and to use this as a starting point for our '#JQAD' journey. We used the QII Report to put action plans in place to get back on track. The staff training/meeting was very positive and the team were buzzing with excitement to move forward together on improving quality and adding impact.*

*I cannot begin to tell you how incredibly amazing Vanessa is ... She has truly transformed my setting. My Manager and Deputy have redistributed their roles and responsibilities to utilise their strengths and the Manager is now going into each room daily to observe, model, guide and support staff. The Impact of the QII has been huge and worth every penny and more!!!*

*If you are needing someone to be brutally honest, highlight the positives, identify the weaknesses and get your team back on track, then Vanessa is the person you need! My only regret is that I didn't know about Vanessa sooner!*

**Jane Deighton, Owner- Little Faces Childcare**

# FINAL WORDS

Thank you for taking the time to read this book. I know there have been many of you who have contacted me to let me know what you think and I am truly honoured to read everyone of them. If you do want to find out more about what we do and how I/we can help you with your inspection on adding impact then please get in touch my email is:

vanessa@jigsaweyc.com.

I did not intend to use this book as a tool to help promote Jigsaw Quality Improvement Inspections but to help you in your upcoming Ofsted inspections.

I often have said during the writing of this... I wish I had this book when I was due an inspection!

And, if you are saying the same, then my mission is complete.

I want you to shine in your inspection and showcase your

setting. It is your one and only chance! And if I can help you with that at all I have succeeded in my mission!

Remember – It is all about IMPACT!

## ACKNOWLEDGMENTS

Firstly, I have to start by thanking Mr D, my husband for being my first friendly critic who has always challenged me to ask myself the question WHY! Over the past eight years, and through the whole writing process, you have always been there to encourage me and be my rock. My world is a better place with you in it. (Slush moment over!)

My children, Emily and Harry, I need you to know how proud I am of what you have achieved. The journey we have travelled over the past eight years has shown you are resilient, strong and beautiful people. You can achieve anything once you put your mind to it. Go and make a difference.

My parents, aka Terry and Joan…. well what can I say. You are my world and I love you both dearly. The role of daughter to parent is continually evolving in our relationship, but this comes with laughter and tears. Simply, thank you for making me who I am!

There are many other people who in my life and through the whole writing process who have helped me along the way. Abi Horne and Sarah Stone, thank you for giving me the push to excel myself and make my dream a reality. The best decision I ever made was to let you into my creation and help me succeed. Thank you, ladies, for helping me put the blinkers on.

And last but not least to the cheerleaders in my life who are constantly putting my crown back on straight when crooked without me knowing. Emma Smith (Topanga) and Carly Craig…You are just the best. And as time moves on so does the amount of support I receive; from old friends to new friends aka 'The Tribe' – you know who you are; You keep me on track and I am honoured to have you in my life. You are constantly encouraging me from the side-lines as you shake your pom poms!

With that comes new additions to the Jigsaw clan, Elizabeth McCarthy and Kate Bennett who provide the stability while my brain goes into over drive – Thank you for being patient with me and I am delighted you are on this journey with me.

Everyone needs a cheerleader or eight in their lives!

Printed in Great Britain
by Amazon

46965488R00132